LOUISIANA PASTIMES

ANCIENT FISHING METHODS, THE HIPPO BILL, A SQUIRREL STAMPEDE *and Other Tales*

Terry L. Jones, PhD

THE
History
PRESS

Published by The History Press
Charleston, SC
www.historypress.com

Front cover, top, left to right: author's collection; author's collection; Free-Images.
com; author's collection; *bottom*: author's collection.
Back cover: Louisiana Division of Archaeology; *inset*: McNeese State University.

First published 2020

Manufactured in the United States

ISBN 9781467145848

Library of Congress Control Number: 2019954261

Notice: The information in this book is true and complete to the best of our
knowledge. It is offered without guarantee on the part of the author or The
History Press. The author and The History Press disclaim all liability in
connection with the use of this book.

To Carol, for putting up with me for forty-three years

CONTENTS

Introduction   7

1. Nothing New Under the Sun   9
2. Alligator Tales   12
3. Last Island's Last Days   15
4. Déjà Vu All Over Again   18
5. Let's Be Careful Out There   21
6. Hippos in the Heartland   24
7. "The Most Impenetrable Jungles"   27
8. Panther Tales   30
9. The Chase Hunters   33
10. Louisiana's Pelican Seal   36
11. Louisiana's Only Fatal Alligator Attack   38
12. The Voyageurs   41
13. The Wreck of the *El Nuevo Constante*   44
14. The Madonna and Matt Dillon   47
15. It Came Out of the Sky   51
16. Louisiana's Early Game Laws   54
17. Squirrel Stampede   57
18. "I Never Saw Such Clouds of Ducks"   60
19. Elk in Louisiana?   63
20. The Next Disaster?   66
21. Catahoula Lake   69

CONTENTS

22. The Flood of '73   72
23. The Wild Girl of Catahoula   75
24. Louisiana's Wild Men   77
25. The First Mound Builders   80
26. Sea Serpents in the Gulf?   83
27. A Shortage of Women   86
28. The Constitution of 1812   90
29. The School of Hard Knocks   93
30. The First Deer Hunters   96
31. Decimation and Restoration   99
32. Is Bigfoot in Louisiana?   103
33. Bigfoot: The Historical Record   106
34. Antoine de la Mothe, Sieur de Cadillac   108
35. The Texas Connection   111
36. Rules for the Road   114
37. The Mighty Red   117
38. The Freeman-Custis Expedition   120
39. The Spanish Touch   123
40. Lost in Paradise   126
41. Historic Hunters   129
42. Old School Hunting   132
43. Deer Hunting Evolution   135
44. The Red River Rapids   138
45. The Great River Raft   141
46. Trailer Trouble   144
47. My Mom   147
48. My Dad   150
49. The Protestant Intrusion   153
50. The Louisiana Maneuvers   156

About the Author   159

INTRODUCTION

Two of my passions are studying Louisiana history and enjoying the great outdoors. I was a Louisiana history professor at the University of Louisiana at Monroe for twenty-five years, and I have spent sixty years hunting, fishing and exploring the Bayou State's woods and waterways.

I also enjoy writing about my interests and have published five books on Louisiana history, including *The Louisiana Journey* (Gibbs Smith, 2007), a popular textbook that was adopted by many of the state's school systems. After enjoying success in the field of history, I became an outdoors writer so I could share my love of hunting and fishing with others.

In 2015, I decided to combine my two passions by writing a monthly column that would focus on Louisiana history and outdoor recreation. Having difficulty in coming up with a title for the column, I asked my wife, Carol, to brainstorm with me, and she suggested "Pastimes." I liked it because the column was going to focus on both past events and leisurely activity. Pastimes was launched and has been enjoyed by the readers of such publications as the *Ouachita Citizen, Country Roads Magazine, Piney Woods Journal, Concordia Sentinel, Louisiana Road Trips, Amite Tangi Digest, St. Charles Herald Guide* and the *New Era Leader*.

The column covers a variety of topics. Some are historical in nature, such as articles on the early exploration of Louisiana, hunting and fishing techniques used by Native Americans and important historic events. Others are based on my personal experiences, including what Carol calls "Terry Moments," or the myriad mishaps that befall me in the outdoors. And there are some articles that are just quirky, such as a two-part story on evidence of Bigfoot in Louisiana, sightings of sea serpents in the Gulf of Mexico and strange things that have reportedly fallen from the sky.

This eclectic mix of topics has proven popular with both readers and my professional peers. The Louisiana Outdoor Writers Association has bestowed its Excellence in Craft Award on several of the articles: "The Chase Hunters" (about the lucrative hunting profession during colonial times), "The Wild Girl of Catahoula" (concerning a mysterious feral woman who terrorized central Louisiana in the late nineteenth century) and "The Great Deer Comeback" (a story on the successful post–World War II deer restocking program, which in this book is titled "Deer Hunting Evolution"). I am also quite proud that another article, "A Shortage of Women," was included in Ric Baker and Vivian Richard Beitman's college-level critical-thinking textbook, *Critical Approaches to Reading, Writing and Thinking* (Kendall Hunt, 2019).

Now, thanks to Arcadia Press, I am able to publish the first fifty Pastimes articles in book form. A number of people have made this possible, and I would like to express my gratitude for their help. Joe Gartrell, Arcadia Press acquisitions editor, guided me through the publishing process, and Rick Delaney's editing improved the manuscript. Patricia A. Threatt of McNeese State University's Frazar Memorial Library provided the Louisiana Maneuvers photo; Valerie Feathers of the Louisiana Division of Archaeology provided images from the division's collection; and Etta Gwynne Shively Smith allowed me to use the photograph of the Shively family preparing for a deer hunt. Thank you all.

1

NOTHING NEW UNDER THE SUN

The Natchitoches area has long been a popular destination for tourists and sportsmen. One visitor from France was especially intrigued at how the local people used trotlines to catch catfish.

The trotlines were, he wrote, "no more than fishing lines about [thirty-six feet] long. All along these lines, numerous other lines are tied about a foot apart. At the end of each line is a fish hook on which they put a bit of… dough or a small piece of meat. With this method they do not fail to catch fish weighing more than fifteen or twenty pounds."

The tourist was André Pénicaut, and he visited Natchitoches three hundred years ago. His journal reminds us that many of our "modern" fishing techniques were actually developed by Indians long ago. The Indians' methods of taking fish were as varied as they were ingenious and would be recognized by any fisherman today.

Hooks and lines were popular, with hooks being made from bone or deer antler and line from deer sinew. Archaeologists have found three-thousand-year-old tear-shaped, polished stones with holes or grooves in the top that are believed to have been weights for nets or trotlines.

The Chitimacha of South Louisiana used wooden slat traps and gill and hoop nets. The latter were made from rabbit vine and were attached to round wooden frames and placed at the mouths of bayous.

The Chitimacha's favorite fishing technique was to swim underwater with small nets made from hemp. These nets were about three feet long and three feet in diameter and had elastic green cane fixed on each side to serve as a spring.

Some modern fishermen continue to practice the old tactic of gigging, or spearing, fish. *Author's collection.*

A number of men lined abreast across a long pond and then swam underwater, keeping their nets open in front of them by pulling the green cane back with both hands. The men stayed underwater until they either ran out of breath or their nets were full of fish. When the nets were full, they let go of the cane, and it sprang shut to close the opening.

One Frenchman who participated in this type of fishing wrote: "I have been engaged half a day at a time…and half drowned in the diversion— when any of us was so unfortunate as to catch water snakes in our sweep, and emptied them ashore, we had the ranting voice of our friendly posse comitatus, whooping against us, till another party was so unlucky as to meet with the like misfortune. During this exercise, the women are fishing ashore with coarse baskets, to catch the fish that escaped our nets."

Spearing fish with harpoons or bows and arrows was also quite effective, with Indians sometimes using torches to hunt at night. Harpoon shafts were usually made from ash, cypress or willow because they float. When a hit was made, the fish quickly became tired from dragging the buoyant shaft across the surface, and if the fisherman missed he could retrieve his harpoon.

My Uncle Preston Copeland told me stories of doing the same thing as a kid on Corney Creek with a carbide lantern and gig. And several years ago, I accompanied Terry Crum and his Fort Necessity friends on a gar-gigging expedition in the Mississippi River. Just like Indians of old, Crum and his friends hurled cypress-shafted harpoons into the gar and then retrieved them once the fish grew tired.

The Choctaw and other tribes sometimes made poison by pounding up buckeyes, green walnuts and hickory nuts and mixing it into the water. The poison affected the fish's gills and suffocated them. Once they floated to the top of the water, the Indians scooped them up by hand.

Growing up in Winn Parish, I knew a number of people who used buckeyes to poison fish (illegally) in Big Creek and Dugdemona River, but I never witnessed it personally.

An alternate method to suffocating fish was to muddy the water by having people stomp through a shallow pool and stir up the thick bottom sediment. One Spanish explorer in Mississippi wrote that the Indians "roiled the water with the mud of the waters and the fish, as if stupefied would come to the surface, and they caught as many as they wished."

My mother recalled going to barrow pits near her Mississippi home during the Depression and using the same method to catch fish. Her father put on rubber boots and churned up the mud while she and her siblings scooped up the small bream that came to the surface.

When it comes to fishing, there's truly nothing new under the sun.

2

ALLIGATOR TALES

L ouisiana has long captured America's imagination with its beautiful bayous, delicious cuisine and abundant wildlife. Television shows such as *Swamp People* have only increased that interest—particularly in Louisiana's famous alligators.

Stories about the alligator (or "crocodiles," as the French called them) began to appear in print soon after the Sieur d'Iberville established the Louisiana colony in 1699. In fact, one of the first mentions of our alligator can be found in Iberville's diary. While exploring Bayou Manchac, he wrote: "We see a large quantity of crocodiles. I killed a small one, eight feet long. They are very good to eat."

André Pénicaut accompanied Iberville on the expedition, and he claimed that the Riviere-aux-Chiens was one of the first places the French named, "because a crocodile ate up one of our dogs there." This stream is probably modern-day Riviere aux Chenes, which forms the western boundary of St. Bernard Parish.

Le Page DuPratz, another early explorer, frequently mentioned the alligator in his memoirs. According to DuPratz, the reptiles were not only widespread but also downright huge. "Among other things I cannot omit to give an account of a monstrous large alligator I killed with a musquet ball.... We measured it, and found it to be nineteen feet long, its head three feet and a half long...at the belly it was two feet two inches thick....M. Mehane told me, he had killed one that was twenty-two feet long." If Mehane's gator was measured accurately, it would have broken the current world record of nineteen feet, two inches.

The author of an 1854 article in *Harper's New Monthly Magazine* also commented on the large size of the gators. He claimed a skull was found with jaws that opened up five feet and that a man once killed an alligator in Pascagoula Bay that measured twenty-one feet long. The writer also mentioned that the famous painter James J. Audubon killed one in the Three Rivers area that measured seventeen feet.

This same author claimed that the alligator's ability to survive long periods of time without food "almost exceeds belief." While living in Concordia Parish, he received a letter from a European scientist requesting a live alligator to study. The author put the word out, and gators soon started arriving at his doorstep—literally. In the dead of night, a neighbor tied to his porch an alligator "whose huge jaws…opened wide enough to swallow any philosopher who would dare to interfere with his habits or dental fixtures."

He finally acquired two alligators he thought would fit the scientist's needs and simply put them in a crate with air holes and shipped them to Europe. Traveling by steamboat and train, it took the critters nearly five months to reach their destination. They arrived in good condition even though "in all that time, lived on else than faith, sunshine, and the dews of heaven."

Louisiana alligator. *Author's collection.*

In the eighteenth and nineteenth centuries, alligators seemed to have flourished all over Louisiana, but writers frequently mentioned their abundance in Red River. One author quoted Audubon as saying the number of gators there was "almost beyond conception. He says he has seen hundreds at once, the smaller riding on the backs of the larger, groaning and bellowing like so many mad bulls about to meet in fight."

In 1876, manufacturers in New York and New Jersey began purchasing Louisiana alligator skins to make boots, shoes and purses, and other companies bought alligator oil for use in machinery. As a result, professional hunters started killing large numbers of the reptiles. On June 3, 1882, the Lafayette *Advertiser* reported, "Three persons residing in the parish of Assumption, last year killed 9000 alligators, saved the oil and sold the hides. The price of the hides is seventy-five cents apiece."

The Department of Wildlife and Fisheries estimates that from 1880 to 1933 approximately 3.5 million Louisiana alligators were killed for their skins (an average of 64,815 per year). The number dropped significantly to 414,126 (18,005 per year) between 1939 and 1960. A growing concern that the Louisiana gator might be killed to extinction led officials to initiate a statewide ban on hunting alligators in 1962.

Ten years later, the gator population had rebounded enough that a commercial season was reopened. Today, thanks to conservation efforts, there are probably more alligators in Louisiana than there were one hundred years ago.

3

LAST ISLAND'S LAST DAYS

August can be cruel. In modern times, it has spawned hurricanes Camille, Andrew and Katrina that devastated Louisiana and killed hundreds of people. An equally destructive, but lesser-known, storm was the 1856 hurricane that destroyed Last Island.

Last Island, or Isle Dernière, was the westernmost, or "last," island in the Gulf's Timbalier barrier chain. It stretched more than twenty miles and had beautiful white sand beaches, gaming establishments and a village of about one hundred houses. Last Island also was home to the Trade Wind Hotel, a swanky resort frequented by New Orleans' upper class.

In early August 1856, hundreds of guests were enjoying the island when the Gulf began to act strangely. People noticed that the water seemed to have a bulge on the horizon and that the "bump" was moving closer to shore.

The bulging horizon was caused by a hurricane, and it was moving north. As the storm approached, the seas around Last Island became heavier. The ferocity of the waves fascinated the vacationers, and they stood for hours watching them crash onto the beach. Robert McAllister, a young Presbyterian minister, wrote, "We did not know then as we did afterwards that the voice of those many waves was solemnly saying to us, 'Escape for thy life.'"

One man reported that on August 9 "a roaring noise was heard in the distance, and the cattle continued for hours walking nervously to and fro around the enclosure, and lowing in a plaintiff way." A blood-red sun set that evening, and the sky had a strange greenish hue.

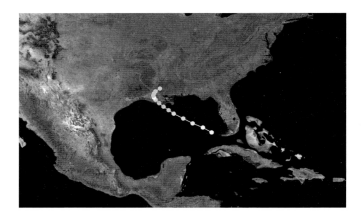

The hurricane of 1856, its track shown here, devastated Last Island and much of South Louisiana. *Wikimedia Commons*.

According to legend, the guests of the Trade Wind Hotel ignored the warning signs and enjoyed a dance that night. By noon the next day, the wind and waves had increased in fury and rain was pounding the island.

The *Star*, a ship that serviced Last Island, was scheduled to dock, and a number of people planned to take it back to the mainland. But the *Star* was unable to reach the island, and the now-worried vacationers realized they were trapped.

When the unnamed hurricane slammed ashore about 4:00 p.m. on August 10, a storm surge swept over the island and carried away most of the people and buildings. One survivor wrote, "Men, women and children were seen running in every direction, in search of some means of salvation."

McAllister and his friends sought shelter in a house, but the roof suddenly flew off, and the four outside walls gave way. Surprisingly, no debris fell on them. "Nothing could fall," McAllister explained. "Everything that was in motion went horizontally."

Realizing they had to escape the rising waters, the small group crawled on all fours across a walkway to a nearby levee, where they held tight to the wooden frame of a derelict windmill. They spent the long night dodging logs and other debris that rushed toward them in the swirling water. On one occasion, a waterspout touched down and spun the wooden frame on which they clung around the windmill's metal pipe.

By dawn it was over, and McAllister and his fellow survivors began walking toward the village. The scene that greeted them was shocking.

"The jeweled and lily hand of a woman was seen protruding from the sand, and pointing toward heaven; farther, peered out from the ground, as if looking up to us, the regular features of a beautiful girl....And, more affecting still, there was the form of a sweet babe even yet embraced by the stiff and bloodless arms of a mother."

The entire island had been swept clean, and there was no trace of the Trade Wind Hotel. Of the one hundred or so houses, McAllister reported, "Not one was left, nay not a sill nor sleeper, not any part of their foundations to indicate that buildings had once been there."

It is believed that the Last Island hurricane was a Category 4 with 150 mile-per-hour winds. Estimates of the death toll range from 140 to 320, with some of the bodies being washed six miles inland. Among those killed were the state's lieutenant governor and the speaker of the house.

The Last Island hurricane also dumped more than thirteen inches of rain on New Orleans, flooded Plaquemines Parish, destroyed every house in Abbeville and sank the steamer *Nautilus* with eighty-six people on board. The sole survivor managed to cling to a cotton bale and float ashore.

When the water drained off Last Island several days later, rescuers found that the storm surge had stripped away all of the vegetation and split the island into the five smaller ones that today are known as the Isles Dernières.

4
DÉJÀ VU ALL OVER AGAIN

The head of the U.S. Fish & Wildlife Service declared in a news release that the "great game of hoarding" ammunition by "greedy individuals" was unsportsmanlike. "I hope that all outdoor writers will make an appeal to good sportsmanship and fair play, and start a campaign to get local sports groups to collect these large ammunition stocks and redistribute them equitably."

During our ammunition shortage, hoarding and speculation seemed to be commonplace, but the situation is not unprecedented. In fact, the federal official's comments were made seventy years ago.

Soon after the United States entered World War II, the federal government began rationing food items, gasoline, tires and even civilian ammunition to make sure our military forces could be properly supplied. The War Production Board (WPB) had the responsibility of regulating all manufacturing and converting the nation to a war economy. Priorities were set, raw material allocated and the production of consumer goods severely restricted.

Ammunition quickly disappeared off store shelves as the WPB curtailed the production of ammunition for civilian use. One year after Pearl Harbor, the nation's domestic ammunition supply was just one-sixth of normal levels. During the 1942 hunting season, the Hutchinson, Kansas *News Herald* declared: "Shotgun ammunition is becoming a rare commodity everywhere, and in the areas where the hunters have been converging the shells for 12 and 16-gauge guns have long been gobbled up....One of these

The World War II ammunition shortage created a strict rationing system for hunters. *Author's collection.*

days you won't be able to get any [ammunition] unless you promise to use it on a Jap or a Nazi."

The ammunition shortage worsened in 1943 when rationing was at its height. In Missouri, the Jefferson City *News and Tribune* reported that the near record squirrel crop might go unharvested because there were no .22 bullets to be had. "As a matter of fact," the paper noted, "most retail dealers simply do not have any ammunition in stock and have been unable to get any."

In August, the *San Antonio Light* warned its readers that there might not be any ammunition for the Texas hunting season. "Although the WPB has announced that ammunition will be released, the dealers generally appear to be about as trusting as the general public has learned to become of bureaucratic announcements of what is to be and what isn't to be."

"Some dealers apparently cling to the hope there will be a pot of ammunition at the feet of the promissory rainbow, but most of them are frankly bearish."

The WPB did not finalize its 1943 civilian ammunition policy until September, when it announced that rationing would be based on how much ammunition sportsmen already had on hand. Each person had to sign an affidavit stating he did not have in his possession more than one hundred rounds of .22 rimfire ammunition, twenty rounds of centerfire and fifty shotgun shells. He then could purchase fifty rounds of rifle ammunition and twenty-five shotgun shells. Dealers were required to keep records of all sales.

The WPB used a quirky formula based on the number of hunting licenses issued and the estimated population of game and predatory animals in each state to determine how much ammunition to distribute. Louisiana's 1943 allotment was recommended to be 2 million shotgun shells and twenty-five thousand rounds of rifle ammunition.

Northern deer hunters were dismayed to learn that the WPB refused to allow the production of any shotgun slugs. Many northern states allowed deer hunters to use only slugs, and the government's ban did not bode well for the upcoming season.

New York's conservation commissioner made a public appeal to hunters to share their ammunition because many families depended on wild game to supplement their meager food rations. "Unless the more fortunate hunters are willing to release a few shells from their extra supply, hundreds of war workers throughout the state will be unable to participate in the game crop harvest at all this fall."

Louisiana's conservation commissioner, Joseph L. McHugh, echoed this sentiment. He declared, "One thing is certain, the amount of ammunition available to hunters for the coming season is going to be such that every hunter will have to use it carefully and those who have stocked up large supplies should share them with others."

The government ended ammunition rationing two months after Japan surrendered, but sportsmen continued to experience shortages. Mississippi's *Hattiesburg American* announced on October 31, 1945, "Production is increasing but it will take some time to swing-over to large scale output of civilian-type ammunition."

Today, the ammo industry seems to be catching back up with demand. But if a shortage occurs again, be patient—history has shown us it could be worse.

5

LET'S BE CAREFUL OUT THERE

It seems that every year when hunting season kicks into high gear, we read of some sad accident that befalls a hunter. Truth be told, I've had my own painful and embarrassing mishaps. It's usually my own fault, but those experiences have taught me a lot about the dos and don'ts of playing in the outdoors.

I am fairly intelligent and reasonably coordinated, with a healthy dose of common sense. However, strange accidents just seem to happen to me; so much so that Carol, my wife of forty-three years, has come to call them "Terry Moments."

Statistically, the most dangerous part of hunting is driving to the woods, but, as they say, I never studied statistics. It's sometimes a challenge for me to just get out of the driveway.

For example, a few years ago, I was loading my four-wheeler into the truck bed before daylight. As I goosed it a bit to get all the way in, the ramp went flying out from under me. The back wheels dropped off the tailgate, and the machine began falling over backwards on top of me.

Luckily, the ATV got hung up on the tailgate, and my only injuries were some scrapes and bruises sustained as I tumbled to the driveway. The lesson I learned that morning is to always make sure that the ramp's safety cables are firmly attached to the truck.

Tree stands have also tried to kill me in the past—twice.

I bought my first ladder stand some thirty-five years ago and was excitedly putting it together on the living-room floor. When I found a bolt was missing, I looked in our junk drawer for another but couldn't find one. Not to worry,

Falling out of a deer stand is just one of the author's "Terry Moments." *Alissa Zeringue, author's collection.*

I thought, I'll just attach the step with a large nail and bend it back to hold the step in place. Carol looked up from her magazine in disbelief and asked, "You think that's a smart thing to do?"

"It's just until I can get another bolt," I assured her.

It was still dark on opening morning when I leaned my new stand against a tree and climbed up to attach it. I had entirely forgotten about the nail— until I reached the fourth step. Suddenly, the nail straightened, the step came off, and I slipped through the ladder and got hung up. The stand then slowly began falling away from the tree.

It's amazing the mental clarity one has in that nanosecond between realizing you've really screwed up and the moment of impact. "That wasn't very smart" flashed through my mind first, followed by, "I wonder how bad this is going to hurt."

Chiropractors and heavy meds helped me recover from the wrenched neck, but I did learn that there are rare occasions when one should listen to the wife.

Two years later, same leaning stand (with a new bolt), same area. This time, I got it successfully placed against a beech tree next to a dry creek bed. After hunting for about an hour, I shifted my weight, the stand twisted and I went over the side.

I hit the creek bottom with a thud, like a head-shot fox squirrel. My loaded .30-06 landed next to my head with the muzzle in my face.

I learned two things that day. Safety harnesses do little good unless you actually wear them, and the quality control on Remington 700 safeties must be pretty good.

Never let your guard down, even when the hunt is over. Years ago, when I was going to Louisiana Tech, my brother Danny and I often bow hunted on the Jackson-Bienville Wildlife Management Area (WMA). One day, while walking back to the truck, I was taking practice shots at leaves and dirt clods with a field tip.

I had been working on relaxing my grip and was holding the bow with just my thumb and first two fingers. I was at full draw when I learned there is a fine line between a relaxed grip and no grip at all.

"Whack!" The old Fred Bear recurve slipped from my hand and smacked me right in the face. Stunned, I stumbled back to the truck, thankful that there had been no witnesses. Danny, however, immediately pointed to my head and asked, "What in the world happened to you?" Reaching up, I discovered the large goose egg on my forehead and had to explain everything.

Enjoy the outdoors this month, but remember to be careful out there.

6

HIPPOS IN THE HEARTLAND

W e all fantasize about that hunt of a lifetime. Mine would be floating down Bayou Teche on a balmy winter day. Scanning ahead for my quarry, I spot a large bull, snatch up my trusty .375 Holland & Holland double and drop the trophy with a well-placed headshot. My buddies whoop and share high fives as we take photos of the beast and then ponder how to load the four-ton hippopotamus into the boat.

Sounds outrageous? Well, if Teddy Roosevelt and Representative Robert Broussard had their way back in 1910, today's hunters might well have a hippo stamp to fill the freezer with some bayou bacon.

At the turn of the twentieth century, immigration was causing the nation's population to soar, and meat was becoming scarce. Prices were rising so dramatically that many people either boycotted meat out of protest or were forced to limit their consumption dramatically.

To alleviate the shortage, British adventurer Frederick Russell Burnham hatched a scheme to transplant various African animals to the United States to be domesticated for the market and hunted for food. Burnham, a famous British soldier and Africa expert, was the inspiration for both the Boy Scouts and Indiana Jones.

Burnham wrote an article outlining his plan and quickly gained the support of the *New York Times* and former president and hunting enthusiast Teddy Roosevelt.

Robert Broussard, a Louisiana congressman from New Iberia, liked the idea and saw Burnham's plan as a way to kill two birds with one stone. By the early twentieth century, many South Louisiana bayous were clogged with invasive Japanese hyacinths. Japanese delegates to the 1884 New Orleans international cotton exposition had introduced the hyacinths to Louisiana, but they quickly escaped confinement and spread across the lower part of the state.

Broussard was told that African hippos loved to eat hyacinths and that their meat was delicious. Figuring that South Louisiana was a lot like Africa, he believed hippos would easily adapt to our bayous. While they cleaned up the streams, Louisiana's sportsmen could hunt them for meat.

In 1910, Broussard introduced HR 23261, more commonly known as the "Hippo Bill," and held an agricultural committee hearing on the subject. Broussard enlisted Burnham and Fritz Duquesne to drum up interest in transplanting hippos and to raise money from investors.

While Burnham was a well-respected international figure, Duquesne was a rather mysterious con man. A South African Boer, he had fought against Burnham in the Boer Wars and was known as the "Black Panther." Both men had served as scouts and were once issued orders to kill the other, but now the former enemies put aside their differences to work together on Broussard's plan.

Theodore Roosevelt supported the transplanting of hippos to South Louisiana for hunting. *Free-Images.com.*

William Newton Irwin, a researcher for the Federal Bureau of Plant Industry, also supported Broussard when he testified at the hearing. Irwin insisted that hippo meat was quite tasty and that the only reason Americans had not tried it before was "because nobody ever told them it was the proper thing to do."

"Killed under right conditions and cooked properly it is not only good, but it also really is a delicacy. In flavor it is a blend between good beef and turkey. Sometimes one might say it is a combination of beef and fine sweet pork."

Bringing hippos to Louisiana was just one part of the overall plan to end the nation's meat shortage. At Broussard's hearing, experts advocated putting zebras on the Great Plains, giraffes in Virginia and Arizona to provide both meat and leather and white rhinos (whose meat was said to be delicious) in the Desert Southwest. Other animals on the transplant list included yaks, llamas, African buffalo, gemsbok and gnus.

Broussard's hearing elicited support from across the nation. The *Indianapolis Sunday Star* noted: "We have enriched our native stocks of flowers, fruits and vegetables with contributions from all over the world. But we have strangely overlooked the earth's stocks of useful, edible and ornamental mammals. We hope the Louisiana legislature will look into this matter, as requested by its forests, fish and game commissioner, and that congress will pass Broussard's bill."

The *San Francisco Call* wrote, "Lake cow bacon, made from the delicious hyacinth fed hippopotamus of Louisiana's lily fringed streams, should soon be obtainable from the southern packing houses."

Alas, in the end, no hippos ever made it to Bayou Teche. Despite Broussard's hearing and all of the publicity, the Department of Agriculture decided the meat shortage could be better addressed by converting more land to ranching and finding new ways to increase beef production. Perhaps it was for the best. If you think feral hogs are a problem....

7

"THE MOST IMPENETRABLE JUNGLES"

I n October 1907, President Theodore Roosevelt went on a two-week bear hunt in Madison Parish as a guest of future Louisiana governor John M. Parker and Tabasco tycoon and former Rough Rider John A. McIlhenny.

In 1908, Roosevelt published an account of his outing titled "In the Louisiana Canebrakes." He reported, "On the trip, all told, we killed and brought into camp three bear, six deer, a wild-cat, a turkey, a possum, and a dozen squirrels; and we ate everything except the wild-cat." One of the bears was a 202-pound sow that Roosevelt killed in a dense canebrake at twenty yards.

People were fascinated by the planned hunt, and the nation's newspapers frequently reported on it. In an October 6 article, the *San Antonio Light* provided its readers a vivid description of Northeast Louisiana's primeval hardwood forests and the type of hunt the president could expect.

POSSIBLY NO SECTION OF this country so nearly approaches the hunter's paradise as does northeast Louisiana, where the president will take to the woods for two weeks.

The term *swamp* as applied to that section as the descriptive term is usually understood as a misnomer. It is not a swamp in the sense that it is wet, a bog. It is a vast stretch of slightly undulating virgin forest, perfectly dry in the fall season. Its undulating character consist of what are locally known as ridges or sloughs. In the rainy season these sloughs

Today, the Tensas River swamp looks much like it did when Theodore Roosevelt hunted there in 1907. *Author's collection.*

are the natural means of draining the surface water into the natural outlets, which of this section are the Tensas river, Joes bayou and the bayou Macon, the latter being in no sense a bayou, but a beautiful clear, swift flowing river, navigable a good portion of the year. In the fall season these sloughs are open and dry and afford a good, open driveway through the woods. The ridges are slightly elevated sections lying between the sloughs, being covered with vines, briars, heavy timber and the thick underbrush, but not at all impassable for a man on horseback. It is along these ridges that the game, such as deer, turkeys, squirrel, etc., are found in the greatest abundance....

Within a few miles of the hunt club there are several large deadenings, that is, tracts of land upon which the large timber has been killed preparatory to cultivation, but the clearing was never completed. These are the most impenetrable jungles to be found in America. Within the same radius are also several large cane ridges, covered with heavy cane, impassable only in so far as the hunters with their large knives have cut trails through them. It is in these latter described places that the bear, the wolf and the panther have their lair and when the sport of deer hunting becomes too tame the president can find an abundance of larger game in these places. Only last week the negroes killed two large bucks in one field and just a little distant a large bear.

The methods employed in hunting in this section are as follows: Hounds are always used, as it is not considered sportsmanlike to do still hunting. That is too much like murder.

After a daylight breakfast the party will take a part of the hounds into the open swamp, leaving a part at camp in reserve in the event the others run entirely away for the day in pursuit of a deer.

Then it is a game of every man take care of himself and the devil of the hindermost. The cry of the pack as it reverberates through big timber is the sweetest music that can ever strike upon the sportsman's ears. The game in that section is so plentiful that e'er long the pack will be split, divided, and possibly half a dozen deer being run by different dogs....

Much more excitement will be found in bear than deer hunting....His range is bounded by the deadening or canebrake; he does not take to the open swamp, or rarely does, unless it is to go from one brake or deadening to another. With him there is no such thing as "losing the dogs," or getting out of their hearing, but it is a whoop race, hurrah and fight till he is killed....

The president will find a most delightful country and charming people in North Louisiana. He can leave his secret service men behind, as there are no anarchists or people of that sort in that section. They are all either genuine Americans or genuine Africans and all, in their places, whether high or low, patriotic, law-abiding, hospitable citizens.

8

PANTHER TALES

Recently, trail cameras and the killing of a cougar in Bossier City have proven what hunters have known for a long time—there are "panthers" roaming Louisiana's woods. In the old days, encounters with cougars were common and sometimes fatal.

Texas historian J. Frank Dobie wrote about one incident that occurred in the mid-1800s when a local man took advantage of a rare snowfall to go deer hunting on Bayou Macon. When he failed to return home, a search party went out and discovered that the hunter was following a large set of deer tracks.

Eventually, they found the man's mutilated body and determined that a panther had jumped on him when he walked under a leaning oak tree and "sucked blood from his throat." The men trailed the panther another sixty yards and found where it had killed a buck and sucked blood from its throat, as well. They concluded that the panther killed the deer the hunter was trailing and then ambushed him from the tree.

In 1874, the *Galveston Weekly News* carried a story about another panther victim in Northeast Louisiana. A Delta man left home in his wagon and had been gone only fifteen minutes when the wagon team came rushing back home without the driver. Neighbors went looking for the man and found him less than a mile away. "The body of the man was lying in the road, and a huge panther was standing over it, eating one of his shoulders....When they got back (with a gun), the panther was still engaged eating its victim. They fired, but did not succeed in killing it, and the panther ran away into the woods."

Just four years later, the *Ouachita Telegraph* reported on a fatal encounter in western Catahoula Parish. "It seems the unfortunate victim had started to a neighbor's house near by, and in passing through a skirt of woods was attacked by the hideous and dangerous animal. Her husband, becoming uneasy at her long absence, went in search of his wife and when he reached the scene he found the panther devouring its prey. The husband fired at the panther but without effect."

An eerily similar incident occurred nearly thirty years later in the same vicinity when another woman was killed and eaten ten miles west of Columbia. Anna Valentine had also left to visit a neighbor, and her husband began searching for her when she failed to return. He "found his wife's head and her skeleton, picked bare of flesh in a clump of bushes. Bits of the woman's clothing were scattered over a distance of two miles, showing that the panther had dragged its victim to a convenient spot to make a feast."

For decades, newspapers nationwide carried stories about the Louisiana panther.

Nashville Daily Union, May 6, 1866: "Last week a young son of Mr. William Gordy, on lower Bayou Sale, killed a panther eight feet in length. He by mistake gave him a charge of bird shot from a double barrel gun. The panther was in a tree when the lad paid his respects to him."

The Florida panther, or cougar, was once common in Louisiana. *National Park Service.*

Omaha Daily Bee, December 24, 1886: "A Louisiana panther trotted along beside two little children who got lost in the woods for a considerable time, purring like a cat and never offering to harm them."

Fort Worth Daily Gazette, May 15, 1887: "Word has reached here that a colored child, while picking berries on the Daiger place, near Baton Rouge, Thursday evening, was torn in pieces by a wild animal, supposed to be a panther or Louisiana tiger, by no means rare in the swamps of this state."

Panama City News Herald, January 13, 1952: "Heavily armed hunters [near Shreveport] cautiously beat their way through thickly wooded Louisiana hills today in search of a panther that has terrorized this area for two weeks."

Winn Parish Enterprise, 1959: "Stay clear of brier patches in the woods south of Packton. You might stir up a panther's nest, as did Jimmy Wingfield, 16-year-old local youth, while squirrel hunting in the area Saturday afternoon." Young Wingfield was retrieving a bird he shot in a thicket on Caney Creek when the tan-colored panther bolted. He emptied his .22 at it and reported that the cougar "began growling and screaming." Wingfield claimed the cat was as "big as a great Dane dog."

Panthers are incredibly rare in our woods today, and people have nothing to fear from them. If you are lucky enough to catch a glimpse of one, savor the moment.

9

THE CHASE HUNTERS

Hunting was one of Louisiana's most lucrative occupations 250 years ago. Professionals known as "chase hunters" spent as much as a year in the deep woods pursuing deer, buffalo and bear.

Skins and meat were in high demand, and hunting became an important part of Louisiana's economy. By the 1730s, hunters working out of Natchitoches were collecting more than twenty thousand deer skins every few months.

Much of the hunting focused on the upper Ouachita River—what the French called the Black River. The Ouachita Valley was in the Natchitoches district, so merchants there often became partners with the chase hunters.

A 1764 contract between Natchitoches resident Andre Rambin and hunter Joseph Gallien is typical of this arrangement. Gallien was heading to the Ouachita River with a black man and an Indian woman to hunt buffalo, bear and deer for an entire year.

Rambin agreed to furnish Gallien with twenty-five pounds of powder, fifty pounds of musket balls, a flintlock musket, one hogshead of salt, a copper cauldron, twelve butcher knives, fifty gun flints, twelve ramrods, two axes, an adz, a mosquito bar, fifty pots of rum, fifty pounds of flour, twelve pounds of sugar, twelve pounds of rice, three barrels of corn, eight pots of bear oil and three hundred livres to pay the black man.

After the hunt, Gallien was to take all of the skins, bear oil, buffalo liver and tongue and salted meat to New Orleans, where he would divide it with Rambin.

Bear oil was one of the chase hunter's most valuable commodities. *Author's collection.*

Bear oil was one of the most valuable commodities sought by the chase hunters. It was collected by boiling bear meat in a large pot of water and then skimming off the oil as it rose to the top like cream.

The oil was used for lamp fuel and cooking and as a lubricant, a hair and moustache wax, a substitute for olive oil on salads, a leather softener and a body ointment. It was particularly popular in hot, humid Louisiana because it did not turn rancid in the summer like other animal fats.

Bear oil was even used as a form of currency. The oldest document in the Natchitoches courthouse is a 1722 contract between a settler and a carpenter. The settler hired the carpenter to build a house and agreed to pay him partially in bear oil. Another contract shows that a settler sold a house for bear oil.

Hunting was so important to Spain's economy after it acquired Louisiana in 1763 that the governor dispatched Captain Jean Baptiste Filhiol up the

Ouachita River to gather the hunters' families into settlements so they could be protected against roaming bands of Osage and Choctaw Indians.

Filhiol, his wife and a few companions paddled canoes from New Orleans to the Ouachita River. On arrival, Filhiol was horrified at the chase hunters' lifestyle.

He claimed they took no precautions against going hungry and simply lived from hand to mouth on animal meat and some produce that grew haphazardly around their crude lean-to shelters. Starvation was so prevalent that mothers fastened belts tightly around their crying babies to help stifle the hunger pangs. (Filhiol never explained why professional hunters in a hunting paradise were constantly hungry.)

Mothers also had a peculiar way to keep their toddlers occupied while they went about their work. Filhiol claimed they tied a short piece of string to a chunk of bear fat and fastened the other end to the baby's big toe. The child was then left on the ground, where it was content to gnaw on the bear fat for hours.

When the baby inevitably swallowed the greasy meat and began to choke, it would instinctively kick, and the string to the toe would pop the meat out of its throat.

Filhiol reported that the hunters lived a life "of the greatest independence, placing work in horror, knowing hardly if they were Christian, who will, whenever they find occasion, make joy out of incest, of whom perjury, intoxication, and adultery pass as niceness."

Filhiol eventually established the Poste du Ouachita on an open prairie known to the locals as Prairie of the Canoes because hunters often gathered there. When the Indians continued to threaten the people, Filhiol built Fort Miro in 1791, and it became the seat of government for the Ouachita district. The settlement at Fort Miro was renamed Monroe in 1819 to honor the *James Monroe*, the first steamboat to go up the Ouachita River.

LOUISIANA'S PELICAN SEAL

Free-Images.com.

It is common knowledge that the pelican is Louisiana's state bird and that it is depicted on our official seal, but many people wonder why. Why would Louisiana choose such a symbol over more impressive animals such as eagles, panthers or bears?

The answer lies with one man.

After the United States bought Louisiana in 1803, the land that would compose our state was named the Territory of Orleans. President Thomas Jefferson appointed twenty-eight-year-old William C.C. Claiborne governor, and the territory's legislative council authorized him to design an official government seal.

Claiborne adopted a seal depicting an eagle holding a laurel wreath in its beak with fifteen stars arranged at the bottom to represent the states of the Union. But after Louisiana became a state in 1812, the seal was changed to a pelican perched on its nest, plucking at its breast to draw blood to feed its ten chicks (oddly, the pelican's head was originally shaped like that of an eagle, or a "condor," as one historian described it). This early seal also had the state's motto, "Justice, Union & Confidence," and eighteen stars representing the states.

Why Claiborne changed the seal from an eagle to a pelican is not clear, but it might have been his way to honor the state's Catholic heritage.

In ancient times, people believed the pelican would tear the flesh from its own body to feed its young in times of famine. Early Christians tapped into this common belief and began using the pelican as a symbol for Christ's sacrifice and blood atonement. As late as 1812, a Catholic prayer book used a pelican as a symbol of self-sacrifice, and it looked identical to the one on Louisiana's 1813 seal.

Today, illustrations of pelicans can still be found in many churches. One is carved into the south porch of the cathedral in Cornwall, England. Another is in a stained-glass window of the cathedral in Bourges, France. And a pelican can be found in the pulpit of the Anglican church at Aldington in Kent, England.

Because the pelican was a familiar symbol to Catholics in the early nineteenth century, its use on the state seal would have made political sense, considering Louisiana was the only predominantly Catholic state at the time.

Although Louisiana's Catholic population was familiar with the pelican's symbolism, its use on the seal was a source of bemusement to others. When word of the seal was brought to Tennessee, the *Nashville Banner* declared, "The people of the new state have strange ideas."

The pelican has continued to be on Louisiana's seal since 1813, although the seal's design has changed. (Many individual state departments also designed their own unique pelican seal.) For example, blood was sometimes shown spurting from the pelican's breast and sometimes not, and the number of chicks in the nest has changed. Thanks to the research of Joseph Louviere, a Houma eighth-grade student, the state legislature passed a bill in 2006 to put the spurting blood back in the flag.

The state motto has also morphed from "Justice, Union & Confidence" to "Union, Justice & Confidence."

Our current state seal was authorized in 1902 to bring uniformity to the various designs, and the pelican flag was officially adopted in 1912, even though it had been in common use long before.

Today, Louisiana's pelicans can be seen in several prominent places. England's famed Westminster Abbey has a stained-glass window depicting the seals of the state of Louisiana and the city of Monroe, both of which contain pelicans. This window was commissioned a number of years ago by former governor James A. Noe's daughter Linda Noe Laine. Louisiana's pelican seal is also depicted in marble mosaic at the west narthex of the Washington Cathedral Episcopal Church in Washington, D.C.

One question that continues to puzzle people is why the white pelican was used for the state seal and flag when the brown pelican is the official state bird. The answer is simple. The white pelican was incorporated into the seal and flag more than two hundred years ago, but it was not until 1966 that the legislature chose the brown pelican to be the state bird.

LOUISIANA'S ONLY FATAL ALLIGATOR ATTACK

A lligator numbers have exploded in the last twenty-five years, but for some reason, attacks on humans are extremely rare in this state. In fact, it is claimed that Louisiana has never experienced a fatal gator attack, but that may be incorrect. A 1734 coroner's inquest at the French outpost of Fort St. Jean Baptiste in Natchitoches concluded that an alligator killed one of the local residents.

About 7:00 a.m. on August 10, a slave woman informed coroner Jacques de la Chaise that there was a nude body lying on the bank of Red River (modern-day Cane River). De la Chaise, Father Vitry and a handful of other men went to the river and found the body of Jacques du Bois, the fort's blacksmith, lying half in the water.

De la Chaise wrote in his coroner's report: "We found near the ear, three wounds equally distant from [illegible]. In addition to this, we found the eyes bulging and unusually swollen. We did not notice any other wound on the rest of the body, which led us to believe an alligator had attacked him while he was bathing, since we found the body nude."

Whenever someone died at Fort St. Jean Baptiste, it was customary to inventory all of their possessions. If there was no heir, a series of drum rolls called the local people to the fort for a public auction of the goods.

Jacques du Bois was a bachelor who lived in a single room supplied by his employer, fort commandant Louis Juchereau de St. Denis. His property inventory provides a glimpse of what a working-class bachelor possessed in colonial Louisiana.

Stored in a small locked chest were two shirts and a pair of pants (all described as being "half worn out"), a coat, four pairs of stockings worn out at the feet, an old cap lining, a pair of linen pants, a "worn-out" tie and a promissory note for fifty-eight livres signed by a soldier nicknamed La Fleur ("the flower"), of which thirty-five livres were still due. Elsewhere in the room, the officials recorded the following:

Two worn-out shirts
A worn-out linen suit
An old knife with a deer horn handle
An old handkerchief
A pair of Spanish garters
A suit of thick cloth
A small, faded blacksmith's apron
A half worn-out hat
An old waistcoat
Two leather pillows
Two old leather aprons
A worn-out cap lining
Two glass bottles
A davit (a crane-like device used to hoist cargo onto a ship)
An old open mirror
Two bad pairs of shoes with an old pair of steel buckles
A powder gun with a powder horn
A bad cap made of platille
Two bad barrels from saddle pistols
An iron tobacco box
A coat and breeches made of ticking
An Indian basket
Two old Indian jars
A bunch of onions

The worn-out clothing and meager belongings indicate that Jacques du Bois was not a man of much means. Nonetheless, his fellow settlers came to the fort when the public auction was held and snatched up everything.

In all, the auction brought in 116 livres, and the money was used to pay off the blacksmith's debts. Included was a debt of a little more than 11 livers that Du Bois owed for milk (the document's literal translation has the debt being owed to the cows themselves). Father Vitry was paid 9 francs

Louisiana's only fatal alligator attack occurred in 1734. *Author's collection.*

for burying du Bois, the fort's drummer received 3 francs for announcing the auction and the fort's clerk was paid 3 francs for removing the body from the river bank. Just over 8 francs were used to pay for inventory and auction expenses.

Although we cannot be certain what caused Jacques du Bois's death, if an alligator did kill him that hot August morning, he must have been the unluckiest Louisianian ever to go skinny-dipping. Du Bois is the only person in more than three hundred years of recorded Louisiana history whose death was officially attributed to an alligator.

12

THE VOYAGEURS

Bayous, lakes and rivers have long served as Louisiana's economic highways. Today, diesel-powered tugs push strings of barges up and down our innumerable waterways. But long ago, commercial boats were moved by a colorful set of men known as voyageurs.

Voyageurs (VOY-uh-jurs), a French term meaning "travelers," were professional boat paddlers who were usually employed in the fur trade business.

Paddling cypress dugouts (or birch bark canoes in the far North) was a physically demanding job, and it required the hardiest of men. One Jesuit priest who traveled with the voyageurs wrote that they "are not scared to paddle five or six hundred leagues [1,250–1,500 miles] in a canoe, or live for a year or eighteen months on corn and bear fat and sleep under shelters made of rocks or branches."

Everyone who rode with the voyageurs was astonished at their stamina and disdain for rest. After paddling for sixteen hours, one group was asked if they wanted to stop for the night. "They answered they were fresh yet," reported one man. "They had been almost constantly paddling since 3 o'clock this morning….57,600 strokes with paddle, and 'fresh yet!' No human beings, except the Canadian French, could stand this. Encamped at half past nine o'clock, having come today seventy-nine miles."

Because dugout space was at a premium, voyageurs were required to be short in stature so as to not take up much room. But they possessed

Louisiana's early economy depended on voyageurs to move goods across the colony. *Painting by Charles Deas, Boston Museum of Fine Arts.*

tremendous upper-body strength and endurance. Voyageurs had to make approximately one paddle stroke per second for at least fourteen hours a day and be able to carry several hundred pounds of cargo on their backs during portages.

Long trips settled into a predictable routine, with the voyageurs normally eating just breakfast and supper and rarely stopping to rest. Meals usually consisted of corn or peas and grease, or pork or bacon stewed up in a kettle. The meat gave rise to the voyageurs' nickname, *mangeur de lard* ("bacon or pig fat eaters"), which is also where we get the word "lard." When the voyageurs were in a hurry, they simply poured out their gruel, got down on all fours and lapped it up like dogs.

One of the most difficult jobs for the voyageurs was to portage around obstacles such as logjams or the Red River rapids at modern-day Alexandria. Trade goods, furs and supplies were stored in ninety-pound bundles, and voyageurs were expected to strap on two at a time, carry them about a third of a mile and then set them down and go back for two more. After relaying the bundles through the portage, they had to go back and carry or drag the dugouts forward.

Voyageurs took pride in their physical abilities and considered it unmanly to complain of the hardships. They also had a fierce competitive spirit and often challenged one another to paddling and portage contests. Witnesses to such events reported incredible feats of strength. Some voyageurs are said to have strapped on 720 pounds during portages, and a few died after suffering ruptures from carrying such heavy loads.

Voyageurs were generally fun-loving men who enjoyed eating, joking, singing, smoking and gambling. These extraordinary characters were described as always being polite, especially toward women and one another. They created their own peculiar culture with distinctive dress, customs and traditions, and most of them had nicknames that were the opposite of their appearance or character. *La Petite Vierge* (little maiden), for example, was a huge man, and *Wapishka* (white) was black.

On the river, voyageurs paid little attention to cleanliness, but they always freshened up and put on their finest clothing before reaching an outpost so they could impress onlookers (especially women). One American wrote, "On Sundays, as they stand round the door of the village churches, they are proud dressy fellows in their parti-coloured sashes and ostrich-feathers."

Voyageurs also adorned themselves with a wide variety of jewelry and wore silver broaches, earrings and crosses, and silver and brass rings that would rival any "bling" today. Tattoos were particularly popular and included both European and Indian styles in a variety of colors.

Sadly, today there are virtually no reminders of Louisiana's voyageurs. But had it not been for their courage and incredible stamina, the French could not have maintained their colony here. Famous fur trader John Jacob Astor perhaps gave the voyageurs their greatest compliment when he declared that he would rather employ one French voyageur on a trade mission than three Americans.

THE WRECK OF THE *EL NUEVO CONSTANTE*

In 1979, Curtis Blume, a shrimper out of Port Bolivar, Texas, was trolling his nets off the Rockefeller Wildlife Refuge in Cameron Parish when he snagged some unusual copper ingots. Realizing he had discovered a shipwreck, he and some friends began investigating the site and recovered more copper ingots, as well as some gold and a cannon.

Research revealed that the shipwreck was the *El Nuevo Constante*, one of many Spanish vessels that plied Gulf waters in the eighteenth century. At that time, Spain's Mexico colony produced tons of gold, silver and other products that were regularly sent across the Atlantic Ocean aboard ships like the *Constante*.

A manifest discovered in the Spanish archives revealed that the *Constante* was an ordinary cargo vessel and not a treasure ship, as Blume and his colleagues had hoped. Besides gold, silver and copper, it also carried cow and goat hides, indigo, vanilla beans, chocolate, ceramic bowls, medicinal plants, dyewood and cochineal (used in making dye).

With five other cargo vessels and a protective warship, the *El Nuevo Constante* set sail from Veracruz on August 21, 1766, with seventy-one passengers and crew. All went well until September 1. That night, according to one of the ship's pilots, a storm lashed the fleet and had "such bad symptoms that it grew by the instant and became strong hurricanes and unimaginable seas."

The fleet was battered for several days, and the vessels finally drifted apart as they lost masts and rigging. The *Constante* stood the storm well until it

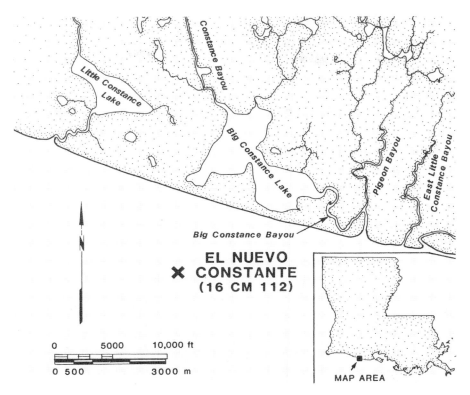

Big Constance Bayou is a reminder of the *El Nuevo Constante* shipwreck. *Louisiana Division of Archaeology.*

began to leak on the night of September 3. Despite heroic efforts to pump out the water, it was settling by the bow when dawn broke on September 5. Some of the heavy cannons were heaved overboard to lighten the vessel, but it did no good. Realizing his ship was sinking, the captain turned north and ran it aground in ten feet of water just more than a quarter mile from the Cameron beach. Amazingly, all of the passengers and crew survived the harrowing ordeal.

When the storm finally subsided two days later, the Spaniards set up camp onshore, and a few men took a small boat to try to get help. They made their way eastward 180 miles to Balize, near the mouth of the Mississippi River, and made contact with Spanish officials.

A rescue operation soon arrived to retrieve the stranded men and salvage the *Constante*, but the Spanish were able to recover very little of the cargo. In a short time, the wreck site disappeared from memory.

After Blume rediscovered the wreck in 1979, Louisiana officials forced him to turn over the artifacts to the state, and Coastal Environments Inc. of Baton Rouge was contracted to conduct a professional excavation.

After 214 years of coastal erosion, however, the wreck was now almost a mile offshore in nineteen feet of water that was so murky that divers could not see their hands in front of their faces. The salvage job was nerve-racking because the divers were constantly in danger of being entangled in fishing line that had broken off on the wreck. They also sometimes sensed (but did not see) large fish swimming nearby.

Among the hundreds of artifacts collected were more than eighty pounds of silver, fifty pounds of gold and seven thousand pounds of copper. None of the silver or gold discs had any inventory markings, suggesting that they were smuggled aboard in an attempt to avoid paying taxes.

Other artifacts included metal and wood ship fittings, ballast stones, three eight-foot-long iron cannons, intact cowhides, spikes, nails, bolts, cannon shot, anchors and various personal items.

Hundreds of ceramic fragments were also recovered, many in the shape of miniature shoes, dogs, llamas, ducks and guitars. These were probably gift items, much like the knickknacks modern tourists buy at roadside stands.

Apparently in honor of the ship, the Spanish named a nearby waterway Bayou del Constante, but over the years its name became corrupted into Constance Bayou. Modern maps of the Rockefeller Wildlife Refuge still show Big and Little Constance Bayous and Big and Little Constance Lakes. They are the sole reminders of the only Spanish shipwreck ever discovered in Louisiana waters.

14

THE MADONNA
AND MATT DILLON

Summer is the time to travel, and Carol and I often take a vacation this time of year. We have fond memories of taking a cruise to Alaska, flying to Hawaii and driving across most of the continental United States.

Although we have visited nearly every state, I have to say that the West fascinates me the most. Its beauty is awe inspiring, and on one occasion we witnessed a true miracle.

Carol and I were in southern Utah visiting the Arches, Bryce Canyon and Canyonlands National Parks. This particular afternoon found us driving down a lonely stretch of road, quietly enjoying the scenery and listening to an oldies station.

Then I saw it. There on the shoulder of the road sat a small statue of the Virgin Mary.

I zipped past her pretty fast, and it took a few seconds for my brain to register what I had seen.

"Did you see that?" I asked.

"What?"

"Back there. There was a little statue of the Madonna sitting on the side of the road."

"You mean one of those shrines where someone was killed in a car wreck?"

"No, it was just a statue about a foot tall."

"A statue of Mary was sitting on the shoulder of the road. A statue of Mary, the Madonna?"

The vast emptiness of the American West can play tricks on your mind. *Author's collection.*

"Yes, just a statue of Mary. There was nothing else around it. It must be some sort of local custom."

By now, Carol is looking at me with that "bless his heart" expression that husbands know so well, which means I have to turn around to prove that I'm not crazy.

There's not another car within miles, so I make a U-turn, stomp the accelerator and head back to the Madonna.

As we approach the site, I slow down, lean over the steering wheel to get a better look and turn down the radio so I can see better.

"There. There it is."

I point to the shoulder as we pass by and then quickly make another bat turn and head back. The Madonna suddenly drops to all fours and scurries into the sage brush.

"Terry, it's a prairie dog."

"What the…?"

With a straight face, Carol simply says, "Mary moves pretty good."

A few miles down the road, she suddenly points up ahead and yells, "Look, it's St. Peter! No, just a rabbit."

Then, later, Carol said, "There's Gabriel! Wait, it's a tumbleweed."

And on and on and on.

To this day, I can see the Madonna standing on the side of the road. Why she miraculously transformed into a prairie dog remains one of God's mysteries.

What impresses me the most about the West is its vast emptiness. You can often see fifteen miles or more down the road and not encounter another car along the way. In some places, there is not even a tree or a rock or a hill in sight.

On another trip, we were driving through a flat, featureless prairie, and I began to wonder how the pioneers were able to navigate such land. Carol didn't share my curiosity.

"Look at this," I exclaimed, sweeping my hand across the horizon. "There's nothing out there, nothing to take a bearing on. How did people get from point A to point B with no landmarks to go by?"

"I don't know."

"Well, how did the first wagon trains know where to go? Did they use a compass?"

"They might have."

"The ground is packed so hard and the wind blows so much dust, a horse wouldn't leave any tracks. How did posses find outlaws on the run? If I had a horse and you had a horse and I had a two-day head start, how would you find me out here?"

"It'd be tough."

"Okay, let's say you're Matt Dillon and I just robbed the bank. By the time Chester gets word to you and you pack some supplies and tell Miss Kitty goodbye, I have a few hours head start. How would you track me down?"

I know I finally have Carol's attention when she says pensively, "Well…"

After a moment's pause, she said, "I'd go outside town, camp for the night, have a drink and eat some beans, and then come back the next day and say, 'Well, I lost him.'" Matt Dillon she's not.

Get out on the road this summer and enjoy this beautiful country.

15

IT CAME OUT OF THE SKY

I t's raining cats and dogs"—or fish and frogs and birds and....
Have you ever been outside and got caught in one of those monsoon-like downpours Louisiana is famous for? Probably so, but have you ever seen it literally rain "cats and dogs"?

Since ancient times, people have reported strange things falling from the sky. The list includes rocks, fish, frogs, worms, lizards, birds, turtles, snakes, chunks of meat and blood.

And don't think it's something that only happens in faraway, exotic places. There have been several documented cases in Louisiana in which it rained birds, fish and even worms.

In November 1896, the people of Baton Rouge awoke to a clear sky and prepared for a normal autumn day. They did, that is, until a deluge of dead birds fell "out of the blue."

Ducks, catbirds, woodpeckers and other assorted feathered creatures crashed to the streets in heaps. Most of the carcasses were readily identifiable, but some had strange plumage and others resembled canaries. So many birds plopped down that one contemporary account claimed they "cluttered the streets of the city."

One person declared, "Some idea of the extent of the shower may be gathered from the estimate that out on National Avenue alone the children of the neighborhood collected as many as 200 birds."

A similar incident occurred in Winnfield on April 26, 1930. Residents reported hearing "a roaring, whirring sound" in the sky at about 11:00 p.m.

Birds, worms and other strange things have reportedly fallen from Louisiana's sky. *Free-Images.com.*

when "suddenly thousands of beautifully colored birds began to fall to the ground....For two hours birds literally rained down, carpeting the ground with a mass of color that was dazzling." Many were dead; others seemed so weak from hunger and exhaustion that they just fluttered on the ground, unable to fly.

It was speculated that a powerful storm had gathered them up in South and Central America and swept them north. "The colors of the winged visitors from the tropics ranged from scarlet and jet black, yellow and blue grey, to buff and brown. Their size was about the same as the English sparrow, though some were reported to be as large as a small chicken. Sea gulls were even alleged to be seen in the group." Kids collected some for pets, and Boy Scouts gathered dead ones to earn taxidermy merit badges.

Another event occurred on the somewhat foggy morning of October 23, 1947. Customers were enjoying a quiet breakfast in a Marksville restaurant when a waitress rushed in and gasped, "You won't believe it, but it's raining fish outdoors!"

By the time the customers ran outside, the strange rain was over, but fish covered the streets and sidewalks in an area about one thousand feet long by seventy-five feet wide. Some of the fish appeared to be frozen, while others were just cold to the touch. All were said to be "fit for human consumption."

The fish, which ranged from two to nine inches in length, reportedly struck some people who were caught on the streets.

Several newspapers across the nation carried stories of the strange rain. The *Union Bulletin* of Walla Walla, Washington, reported that a Louisiana wildlife official confirmed all of the fish were native to local waters.

The *Logansport (IN) Press* wrote, "There was a rather surprising variety—hickory shad, large-mouth black bass, goggle-eye, two kinds of sunfish, and several kinds of minnows."

If the Marksville story sounds a bit "fishy," consider what happened in Shreveport on July 12, 1961. According to the *San Antonio Light*, some carpenters were roofing a house when they were suddenly pelted by green peaches that appeared to fall from a dark cloud that passed overhead. About the size of golf balls, the peaches drove the roofers to cover.

And then there is the bizarre story covered by Lake Charles television station KPLC in 2007. On July 11, Jennings Police Department employee Eleanor Beal was crossing a street when large clumps of worms began raining down from the sky.

Beal reported, "All of a sudden, things started falling from the sky....When I saw that they were crawling, I said 'It's worms! Get out of the way!' I ran as fast as I could thinking I could get to shelter."

At the time, there was not a cloud in the sky, but a waterspout had been spotted shortly before about seven miles away. It was assumed that the waterspout was somehow associated with the wormy rain, but no one has ever satisfactorily explained these odd events.

16

LOUISIANA'S EARLY GAME LAWS

B y the turn of the twentieth century, Louisiana's waterfowl and game animals were in trouble. Nonstop hunting by people trying to put meat on the table and market hunters supplying venison, ducks and geese to restaurants and deer hides to leather clothiers was pushing some animals to the brink of extinction. Many of these market hunters used huge weapons, known as punt guns, to kill entire flocks of waterfowl.

Biologists estimate that Louisiana's deer population dropped from several hundred thousand in 1700 to an estimated seventy thousand by the early 1900s. In some areas, deer disappeared completely.

In 1912, the Louisiana legislature created the Conservation Commission and tasked it with managing all of the state's natural resources, including minerals, forestry, fish and game. The commission adopted its first game laws that year, and it is interesting to compare them with today's regulations.

For the first time, Louisiana's fish and game were declared to be the property of the state and were not subject to private ownership unless certain laws were followed. The commission also had to approve the release of any game birds (such as pheasants), and the sale of game fish and most game birds and quadrupeds (including deer) was prohibited.

In most places, waterfowl hunting ran from one hour before sunrise to noon, but the commission had the authority to approve "passe shooting" in specific areas from one-half hour before sunset to one-half hour after sunset. If any parish police jury objected to the latter, the commission could withdraw the passe shooting permission for that parish.

All other game birds could be hunted from one hour before sunrise to one hour after sunset but "only from a gun fired from the shoulder without rest." This provision was aimed at market hunters, who often used the huge punt guns.

The dove and wood duck season was set for September 2 until the end of February; geese and other species of ducks from October 2 to February 29; turkeys (gobblers only) and quail from November 16 to March 31; teal, snipe and sandpipers from September 16 to March 31; Florida ducks, commonly known as black mallards, from August 2 to February 29; papaboote (Mexican sand plover) from July 2 to March 31; and woodcocks from November 16 to January 31.

The commission announced that beginning in 1915 there would even be a season for prairie chickens, kildee, pheasants and turkey hens that would run from November 1 to December 31.

Like today, night hunting was prohibited, but bag limits were more liberal. The daily limit was one turkey gobbler; twenty-five ducks, poules d'eau,

Louisiana's first game laws were passed in large part to protect the duck population from commercial hunters using punt guns. *Free-Images.com.*

Mexican sand plovers or doves; fifty snipe; and fifteen of any other game bird. Licensed professional hunters could shoot fifty ducks or poules d'eau per day.

It was also legal to sell ducks, poules d'eau, snipe, geese, brant and rail from the opening day of hunting season until the end of February. The sale of quail, however, was prohibited, which prompted one newspaper to inform its readers, "The man who likes his quail hereafter must get his dog and gun and go out and get them himself, as they can no longer be had at the restaurants and stands."

Hunters enjoyed an exceptionally long five-month deer season with a five-deer bag limit. The season had to include the months of November and December, but the commission had the authority to adjust the season to meet the needs of the individual parishes.

Squirrel season ran from July 2 to the end of February, with a daily limit of ten. Mink, otters, muskrats and raccoons could be hunted, bought and sold from November 1 to February 1, and muskrats could be killed any time they were found within two miles of a levee. All of these animals could also be taken any time they were found to be depredating private land.

Hunting licenses were not a financial burden. Louisiana residents who hunted on their own property or land within the ward in which they lived paid no fee. Hunting elsewhere within one's home parish required a fifty-cent license. A statewide hunting license cost three dollars, and nonresidents paid fifteen dollars. A professional market hunting license ran ten dollars.

Violation of individual hunting laws was not broken down, but penalties were to be no less than $25 nor more than $100 or imprisonment for thirty days, or both, at the discretion of the court.

17

SQUIRREL STAMPEDE

Forty years ago, David Freeman was hunting outside Quitman, Louisiana, when he witnessed one of nature's oddest spectacles—a squirrel migration. As he described it, a "kagillion squirrels" came through the woods, and it took a good fifteen minutes for them all to pass by.

"It was loud," Freeman recalled. "It was kind of like a bunch of black birds in the wintertime. I don't have any idea why they moved but I'll never forget it."

Reverend Lavelle Spillers heard of another migration that occurred in the late 1940s around Sterlington. "Back in the late 70s an old timer that I deer hunted with told me of a time when he saw a squirrel migration across the Ouachita River. He said there were thousands, maybe tens of thousands, of squirrels that swam across the Ouachita. The migration lasted for several days if I remember right. He said they were so thick that he believed a man could have walked across the river on them."

Squirrel migrations are a little-understood phenomenon, but they occurred fairly regularly in the old days, when the number of squirrels was simply staggering.

Naturalist John James Audubon and a companion witnessed one while floating down the Ohio River in 1819. "About one hundred miles below Cincinnati…we observed large numbers of squirrels swimming across the river, and we continued to see them at various places."

"At times they were strewed, as it were, over the surface of the water, and some of them being fatigued, sought a few moments' rest on our long

For reasons unknown, massive numbers of squirrels will sometimes abandon one area and migrate to another. *Author's collection.*

'steering oar,' which hung into the water....The boys, along the shores and in boats, were killing the squirrels with clubs in great numbers."

In the fall of 1852, people in Wisconsin watched an estimated half a billion squirrels scamper across an area roughly 150 miles long by 130 miles wide. The migration lasted a month, and squirrels were even reported running through the open prairie miles from the nearest trees.

Another large migration occurred in September 1881 near Reelfoot Lake, Tennessee. A newspaper reported: "Squirrels are crossing the Mississippi River…in fabulous numbers. They are caught by the dozens by men in skiffs. They enter and pass through cornfields, destroying everything as they go."

Four years later, one of the largest known squirrel migrations took place when a mass of rodents left northeastern Mississippi and headed to Arkansas.

One of several newspapers that reported on the event declared: "They are crossing the Mississippi from innumerable points along a line [twenty-five miles long]. They are travelling in [the] thousands and the people who live along their line of march are killing them with sticks in countless numbers. Enterprising men are following them in wagons, slaughtering as they go, and shipping the carcasses to the nearest market. They seem to have lost all fear of man, and in some instances have attacked hunters."

The most famous squirrel migration in modern times took place in the eastern United States in September 1968. Hundreds of dead squirrels were found on highways, and people reported finding large numbers of drowned squirrels in New York's Hudson River and in the Tennessee Valley Authority lakes around the Smoky Mountains. In a week's time, 117 carcasses were fished out of the Cheoah Dam raceway. A biologist who investigated the event estimated the number of dead squirrels found on the highways to be one thousand times the norm.

No one knows exactly why squirrels move in such massive numbers. The migrations almost always occur in September, and only gray squirrels seem to be involved.

Some biologists have speculated that unknown psychological factors or an unusual flea infestation may cause the migrations, but the most logical explanation is that the squirrels are reacting to overcrowded conditions.

Squirrel migrations often follow a couple of exceptionally successful breeding seasons, so squirrels may instinctively know that the existing food supply will not support their numbers and respond by leaving the region.

Surprisingly, squirrel numbers don't increase in those areas where they migrate to, because apparently few survive the journey. The published accounts of squirrel migrations frequently mention that most of the tree rats drown, die of exhaustion or are killed by people and predators along the way.

Similarly, the areas vacated do not suffer any long-term decline in squirrel numbers. When conditions are favorable, squirrels can have two litters per year, and the population quickly rebounds.

18

"I NEVER SAW SUCH CLOUDS
OF DUCKS"

Although textbooks don't mention it, about half of our forty-five presidents have been avid outdoors enthusiasts. George Washington enjoyed hunting and fishing on his Mount Vernon estate, and Chester A. Arthur once caught a record-setting fifty-pound salmon.

Calvin Coolidge and Herbert Hoover loved trout fishing, Dwight Eisenhower enjoyed fishing and shooting in addition to golf and Jimmy Carter and both Bushes like to fish.

At least two presidents were fortunate to hunt in Louisiana. Theodore Roosevelt's 1907 outing in Madison Parish is well known, but twelve years earlier, Grover Cleveland made national headlines when he duck-hunted for two weeks at Orange Island (modern-day Jefferson Island).

Cleveland was an avid duck hunter, wrote a book on fishing and shooting and, in 1895, accepted an invitation from Joseph Jefferson to hunt on his Orange Island estate. On November 10, the *New York Times* reported on the president's hunt in an article titled "Cleveland as Sportsman."

President Cleveland is equally a devotee of the gun and the rod. Having unusual physical strength, he is able to handle with equal ease the 7½ or 8-pound bird gun for snipe, partridge, and quail, or the heavy 16-pound 8-bore, duck-gun affected by the Carroll Island Club, near Baltimore, where canvasbacks and redheads are thought to be the only birds worth the expense and trouble it costs to take them. Being stronger, larger, and younger than [former President Benjamin Harrison], he can endure far more

President Grover Cleveland.
Library of Congress.

of fatigue and get wet oftener without danger to his health than can his immediate predecessor, though President Harrison is an excellent shot in the field at snipe and quail, and no mean performer with the heavy eight and ten bore duck gun.

President Cleveland first became known to the country generally, the lovers of the brown double-barrel and the brotherhood of crack shots, when he made a trip from Washington to Orange Island, in Southwest Louisiana, the estate of Joseph Jefferson, to enjoy a fortnight of as excellent waterfowl shooting as the United States affords.

"I never saw such clouds of ducks in my life as there were at Mr. Jefferson's place in Louisiana," the President said on his return from his visit there, "and the marshes adjoining were alive with snipe and small wading game birds of every kind." The President had as his boatmen and guides two of the native Creole duck shooters. These men know every bayou and stream along the coast, and in their light dugouts, called "pirogues," they can go anywhere if there is six inches of water under them. They shoot

thirty-six and forty inch long fourteen and sixteen bore double guns, still using percussion caps and loading their guns with paper as wadding for powder and shot....They are capital shots, and with their old-fashioned guns will kill more birds than any amateur will hope to get with the finest modern breech-loader....

Mr. Cleveland is not fond of fine weapons in his hunting battery. He usually shoots American-built guns, his favorite being an eighty-dollar Colt's, twelve-bore; or, if ducks be the game he expects to find, he uses a ten-bore Parker of the hammer pattern. He sometimes uses a twelve-bore Scott hammer gun of the one-hundred-twenty-five-dollar kind.

There are few better duck shots than the President. He usually loads with pretty heavy charges of powder; four and one-half drams of black in his cartridge for duck and an ounce and one-eighth of No. 1 shot on top of the powder he thinks is about the correct thing. He shoots with great deliberation, and usually lets a duck get well up and away before he puts up his gun.

At least this was what he did in Louisiana, for the birds being very abundant and not frightened with being much shot at, gave him plenty of time and all the leisure he wanted. He stands fatigue well, too, coming up sturdily each evening with no sign of being tired, and notwithstanding the heavy charges he shoots, he has no sore shoulders next morning. His sole preventive for this the bête noir [anathema] of persons who have not shot for some time, is a thorough bath, rubbing the "gun shoulder" (the right) hard, and laving it completely in cold salted water. In this way he escapes the usually "tender shoulder" that is the almost invariable concomitant of a ten-bore duck gun and its great charges of powder and shot....

He never drinks spirits on these trips...."I sleep well, and come back to my work as hard as nails."

19

ELK IN LOUISIANA?

I have always been fascinated by what Louisiana was like when French explorers first arrived here more than three hundred years ago. Their journals give colorful descriptions of a land filled with deer, buffalo and bear, and some even include tantalizing evidence that elk might have been among the native species.

The eastern elk subspecies lived throughout much of the eastern United States. According to H.E. Anthony's authoritative *Field Book of North America Mammals* (1935), the elk's native range was between 35° and 50° north latitude. North Louisiana lies a few degrees south of this recognized range.

On the other hand, Dr. Lyle St. Amant's *Louisiana Wildlife Inventory and Management Plan* (1959) claimed there might have been a moderate number of elk in the state's heavily forested regions.

If elk were here, their remains should be in prehistoric Indian sites. I checked with several of the state's archaeologists, and none of them had ever excavated elk bones during their careers. However, a couple did have vague recollections of hearing about elk bones being found in an Indian site.

The journals of French explorers are our best primary sources for identifying which animals were encountered three centuries ago. Le Page du Pratz was one who specifically mentioned elk.

On a trip up the Mississippi River to the Chickasaw Cliffs (perhaps modern-day Vicksburg or Memphis), du Pratz reported seeing "nothing but herds of buffaloes, elk, deer, and other animals of every kind."

The evidence is inconclusive, but elk may have once roamed North Louisiana. *Author's collection.*

On another occasion, du Pratz visited the rugged region around Natchez and Vicksburg. He described the open meadows and oak and hickory forests in the area and then wrote, "Those rising meadows and tall forests abound with buffalo, elk, and deer, with turkey, partridge, and all kinds of game."

If elk were roaming around Vicksburg, would they have also been found on the Louisiana side of the river? Perhaps. It is known that herds of buffalo grazed on the prairies of Northeast Louisiana, so why not elk?

On one trip up the Ouachita River, du Pratz noted in his journal that he encountered the same animals there that he did in the modern-day Natchez and Vicksburg areas. That would have included elk.

Assuming elk were native to Louisiana, could they be restocked here like they have been in Arkansas? With help from volunteers and the National Park Service, the Arkansas Game & Fish Commission took elk from Colorado and Nebraska in 1981 and successfully relocated them along the Buffalo River in the Ozark Mountains.

Mike Cartwright, Arkansas's elk program coordinator, said: "We approached it from a historical perspective. We knew from the archaeological record that elk were native to Arkansas and we have tried to restore such species of wildlife. Not just elk, but also buffalo, bear, deer and other native species."

In recent years, Arkansas biologists have improved elk habitat by using controlled burns to reduce underbrush and to maintain open fields for grazing. As a result, there are hundreds of elk in Arkansas today, and there has even been limited hunting since 1998.

Despite Arkansas's success, however, Cartwright thinks it would be difficult to duplicate the program in Louisiana. "You need a lot of territory for elk," he explained. "We know they are big movers because of radio collars we have put on some, and they move a lot more than we originally thought."

Cartwright added, "One bull elk we had a transmitter on was found to have a home range of sixty thousand acres."

"You really need a lot of public land to establish elk. One of the problems we have is the elk are beginning to move onto private land, and we're starting to get complaints from landowners."

The largest tract of public land in Louisiana is the 600,000-acre Kisatchie National Forest, but it is divided into several smaller tracts, and its habitat is not conducive to elk. Kisatchie may be great deer habitat with its piney hills, hardwood bottoms and briar thickets, but it lacks the open meadows and grassy regions that are necessary for elk.

"Elk are big grazers, a lot like cattle, while deer browse," Cartwright explained. "Elk need lots of grass and grass-like plants, so they have to have open areas."

As a result, while elk might have once roamed some parts of Louisiana, it is not likely we will ever see them again in the wild.

20

THE NEXT DISASTER?

L ouisiana's Atchafalaya River is unique. A distributary of the Mississippi, it flows out of the Big Muddy near Simmesport and runs approximately 125 miles to enter the Gulf of Mexico near Morgan City. Looking at the broad, turbulent river today, it is hard to imagine that at times in the early nineteenth century people could actually cross it on a fifteen-foot plank.

The Atchafalaya begins in the Three Rivers region, where the Mississippi, Red and Atchafalaya come together. About two hundred years ago, the Red ran into the Mississippi at Turnbull's Bend, and the Atchafalaya ran out of the Mississippi a little farther downstream. A twenty-mile-long logjam at this juncture acted as a dam that allowed little water to trickle down the Atchafalaya's channel.

In 1831, Henry Miller Shreve cut a new channel across the narrow neck of Turnbull's Bend to straighten out the Mississippi so steamboats would have a shorter route into the Red. As part of the "improvements," he also cleaned out the raft that blocked the Atchafalaya.

Removing the logs was like pulling a plug, and the Red suddenly began discharging all of its water down the Atchafalaya instead of the Mississippi. In no time, the minor stream was scoured out and became the wide river we know today.

Shreve's "improvements" also set in motion a chain of events that could one day devastate Louisiana. The Atchafalaya's route to the Gulf is shorter than the Mississippi's, and it has a steeper grade. Because water seeks the path of least resistance, the Mississippi began trying to change course and flow down the Atchafalaya soon after Shreve removed the logjam. It came dangerously close to doing so during the great 1927 flood.

To prevent this from happening, the federal government completed the huge Old River Control Structure near Simmesport in 1963. It diverts all of the Red River and about one-third of the Mississippi down the Atchafalaya while keeping the mighty Mississippi in its channel. During floods, control gates can be opened to allow more Mississippi water to flow into the Atchafalaya and relieve pressure on the Mississippi levees downstream.

So far, the Old River Control Structure has worked as planned, but the massive lock and dam was in danger of collapsing during the 1973 flood. If that ever happens, the Mississippi River will immediately divert down the Atchafalaya, and the consequences will make our modern hurricanes, oil spills and floods seem like minor inconveniences.

It is estimated that about 70 percent of the Mississippi's water would flow through the Atchafalaya basin, weakening or perhaps even collapsing the highway and railroad bridges that cross it. With the loss of U.S. Highway 90 and I-10, east–west traffic would be completely disrupted, creating a traveler's nightmare and higher transportation costs.

The raging water would probably force the abandonment of Morgan City and other basin communities, and the oil and gas wells, pipelines and

If it were not for the Old River Control Structure, the Mississippi River would divert down the Atchafalaya basin. *Author's collection.*

canals would be destroyed. In a replay of the BP disaster, the oil spillage would be immense, and it might take years to repair the damage. Gasoline prices would soar, commercial crawfishing and recreational fishing would be dramatically impacted and the increased sediment and fresh water would ruin the area's oyster beds and shrimp industry.

Such a structural collapse would also cause the lower Mississippi to shrink by two-thirds almost overnight. Constant dredging could probably keep oceangoing vessels moving, but shipping might be interrupted during times of low water.

A more serious problem would be the effect a smaller Mississippi River would have on Baton Rouge, New Orleans and the ecosystem. Because the river's current would be greatly reduced, the Gulf's saltwater would intrude far upstream, killing the vegetation along the riverbank and causing soil erosion. Eventually, the river below Baton Rouge would widen to become a giant saltwater estuary.

Expensive levee systems might protect New Orleans and smaller towns from eroding away, but the communities and industries from Baton Rouge to the Gulf would lose their source of water. Underground aquifers would not be able to fill the need, and multibillion-dollar pipelines would have to be constructed to bring in water.

The implications of an Old River Control Structure collapse are so enormous that it is difficult to wrap one's mind around it. But after Hurricanes Katrina and Rita, the BP oil spill and the floods of 2016, Louisianians have learned that such unimaginable disasters can take place—often in rapid succession. Hopefully, strong measures will be taken to keep the Mississippi River out of the Atchafalaya, but it's hard to stop Mother Nature.

21

CATAHOULA LAKE

Every Louisiana sportsman has heard of Catahoula Lake, the duck-hunting mecca in East-Central Louisiana, but they might not know what a rich and sometimes violent history it has.

Catahoula is a depression lake that was created when seismic activity caused the land to sink, and Little River then filled up the depression with water. It is not known when the lake was formed, but seismic disturbances have been observed in modern times.

On September 23, 1899, Bayou Sara's *True Democrat* reported on one strange event. "All at once bubbles were seen to rise on the surface of the water, the lake appeared to rise in the centre, and for ten minutes waves swept the banks of the lake, the water rising eighteen inches at the time, after which it gradually receded to its original level. This phenomena was witnessed twice the same day."

Archaeological surveys of the Catahoula area have discovered stone spear points that are approximately ten thousand years old, proof that the lake's rich ecosystem has attracted people to its shores since prehistoric times. The name *Catahoula* is, in fact, Indian in origin and may mean "sacred or clear lake" or just "lake."

The most famous Indian story associated with the lake is the origin of the Catahoula cur, Louisiana's state dog. It is commonly believed that it is a result of Spanish explorer Hernando de Soto's wolfhounds interbreeding with native Indian dogs. Modern research, however, has proven that de Soto never entered modern-day Louisiana. Therefore, it

During the summer and fall, herds of deer and cattle grazed on Catahoula Lake's dry bed. *Author's collection.*

is highly unlikely that the Catahoula cur has any connection to the area or the Indians who lived there.

During the Civil War, Catahoula Lake became a dangerous and violent region when the infamous Jayhawkers began hiding out in the surrounding swamps. Jayhawkers were Louisiana Unionists who opposed secession, and they were often joined by Rebel deserters and anyone else who had reason to hate the Confederacy. More often than not, they were little more than bandits who preyed on the local civilians.

One band of Jayhawkers hid out in what is now the Dewey Wills Wildlife Management Area (WMA) between Catahoula and Larto Lakes. An Alexandria resident wrote that these outlaws "entered the residences of planters, carrying off whatever they needed....In remote parts of the parish, they burned buildings."

In February 1864, Confederate authorities sent in the cavalry to drive out the gangs. Their orders were to "hunt the Jayhawkers down with the utmost severity, and shoot any with arms in their hands making resistance."

In writing to two men who lived on Bayou Boeuf, one officer declared: "There are a number of Jayhawkers in the vicinity of Catahoula Lake and Little River, [who are] very troublesome to loyal citizens and defying civil and military authorities. They are difficult to capture only from the fact that when pursued by cavalry they take [to] the swamp."

The officer explained that the cavalry around Larto believed tracking dogs would be helpful in rooting out the Jayhawkers and requested that the men loan their hounds to the army.

Unfortunately, the troopers had little success in capturing the bandits, so shortly afterward, General Camille Polignac, who commanded Confederate troops around Trinity (Jonesville), issued orders that "if Jayhawkers are taken in arms, they will be summarily executed."

When the war ended, Catahoula Lake once again became a tranquil place where private and commercial duck hunters plied their trade. On November 7, 1875, Alexandria's *Louisiana Democrat* reported: "Wild ducks in great quantities have been flying southward over our town the past week. The hunters have been bringing some few from Catahoula lake into market, which are being retailed at 12½ cents each."

On January 21, 1880, the same paper ran a short piece about a duck hunt that three local men had on the lake. They "killed in three shots, and before daylight at that, 66 ducks." There were no game laws at the time, so shooting ducks before daylight was legal, but it would be interesting to know how they managed to find and slip up on the rafting birds in the dark.

Today, the state owns Catahoula Lake, but it is managed by the U.S. Army Corps of Engineers, the U.S. Fish and Wildlife Service and the Louisiana Department of Wildlife and Fisheries. While the western shoreline is privately owned, most of the eastern and northeastern side lies within the Dewey Wills WMA and the Catahoula National Wildlife Refuge. Both allow hunting, fishing and other recreational activities, so sportsmen should be able to enjoy the lake for many generations to come.

22

THE FLOOD OF '73

In March 2016, a one-thousand-year flood event devastated North
Louisiana, only to be followed by a second one in South Louisiana five
months later. When videos of swimming deer found their way onto the
internet, sportsmen began wondering what effect the floods would have on
the herd.

It wasn't the first time high water had threatened the state's deer
population. One of the worst floods to hit Louisiana occurred in the spring
of 1973. So much land went under water that an Oil City, Pennsylvania
newspaper claimed, "If the ocean had treetops sticking out of it, it would
look like Catahoula Parish."

Huge numbers of animals were displaced, and officials took the
extraordinary step of broadcasting corn, oats, soybeans and range pellets in
the Atchafalaya Basin and along the Mississippi River to ensure the stranded
deer would survive.

In Arkansas, several hundred deer became trapped on Montgomery
Island in the Mississippi River. It was believed that the island had the highest
concentration of deer of any river island, with an estimated two deer per
acre. When it was discovered that the deer had eaten all of the available
forage, biologists landed on the island with chain saws and cut down trees
and saplings to provide more browse.

Mississippi seems to have had the most displaced wildlife during the 1973
flood. One Greenville newspaper columnist wrote: "Deer, turkey and other
animals have been reported alongside Miss. Highway 1, both north and

south of Greenville. If you are traveling on this road, watch out for the animals....In spite of the high stage of the Mississippi River, many deer are still on the river side of the levee. Some have found high ground and are sticking it out. I have heard that in some cases, these deer are being fed by members of some hunting clubs."

So many animals sought refuge along the Mississippi River levee that a special task force of agents was formed to protect them from poachers, dogs and well-meaning citizens. C.B. McSwain, an official with the Mississippi Fish & Game Commission, stated, "We wanted to have a display of force for the poachers who might be headlighting or killing deer who are too weak after swimming a long distance to the levee."

McSwain also warned the public that agents were shooting dogs found on the levee without collars so they would not kill the defenseless deer. "Dogs are molesting deer horribly," he declared, although he was unable to give an estimate as to how many deer the canines had killed.

Another major problem Mississippi authorities had in 1973 was well-meaning citizens trying to revive exhausted deer found along the levee in Bolivar, Washington and Issaquena Counties.

"These deer swim for two miles, let's say, and they get on the bank completely exhausted and unable to walk." McSwain reported. "These

The flood of 1973 inundated much of Louisiana. *Author's collection.*

people crowd around them and try to revive the deer. The deer are so shy and wary, they go into shock and could have a heart attack. Many times the deer jumps back into the water and drowns before the horrified eyes of the people who tried to save it."

Despite the dramatic stories, officials did not expect the high water to have much of an impact on wildlife. "What is lost may not be more than what is taken out during a regular season," McSwain reported. "It will be a limiting factor, but certainly not to the extent that it is a detrimental limiting factor."

Authorities in both Louisiana and Mississippi were convinced that few deer actually starved during the 1973 flood. One Mississippi official theorized, "The deer that did die from starvation were probably already in bad shape or stress, and harassment played a part in it."

This same official estimated that only about five hundred out of approximately five thousand deer that became stranded on the Mississippi River levee between Mayersville and Vicksburg died. He also stated that about one hundred deer died of starvation in Louisiana in the Diamond Point area south of Vicksburg.

Jawbone studies revealed that approximately 90 percent of the deer that perished were about one year old. According to the state official, "[The] other deer in the same area were found to be in good shape."

So, when the next inevitable flood comes our way, we should look to the past and take comfort in knowing that Louisiana's deer herd has been surviving such events for thousands of years.

23

THE WILD GIRL OF CATAHOULA

Much like today's Bigfoot sightings, newspapers in the late nineteenth century frequently reported on a mysterious Louisiana figure known as the "Wild Girl of Catahoula." No one ever discovered the Wild Girl's identity, although some speculated that she was the abandoned child of a Gypsy woman who once lived in the area with two young girls. One of the children was reportedly deformed, and the Wild Girl's footprints indicated she had a clubfoot.

The first stories appeared in the early 1880s, and in July 1888, Harrisonburg's *Catahoula News* reported that she had been "causing a great deal of excitement" fifteen miles west of town. The Swilley family claimed the girl snatched up a goose on their farm and then took off into the woods and evaded several search parties.

A month later, two men reported seeing the Wild Girl near Hemp's Creek in LaSalle Parish. The *St. Paul Daily Globe* declared, "They say she is one of the most ferocious-looking beings that the human eye has ever cast upon." The men tried to question her, but she would not let them get near. The newspaper claimed: "She is as fleet as a deer, and at one leap she cleared a root seven feet high. She uses no language, only gibberish."

The men described the Wild Girl as being about sixteen years old, four and a half feet tall with long, beautiful brown hair and weighing 125 to 140 pounds. She carried an old knife and seemed to limp when she walked, although they could not detect a deformed foot.

Once again, a search party was organized to try to capture the Wild Girl, but it was unsuccessful.

Three months later, the St. Martinville *Weekly Messenger* announced that the "'Wild Girl of Catahoula' has turned up again." This time, the witnesses were Captain J.M. Ball and J.C. Goulden, two men of good character who were fishing on Clear Creek near Little River.

Ball claimed that when he heard some nearby hogs squealing as if something had attacked one, he and Goulden investigated. "They soon came to a human being standing on a log with a pig in one hand and a short knife in the other….When she saw the two gentlemen about thirty yards off, she did not seem to be half as much afraid as they did."

The two men backed away from the woman, whom Ball described as "a white female without clothes and would seem to weigh about 140 pounds and as active as a cat….He says she was covered with hair varying in length in different parts of her." The Wild Girl finally ran off through the woods with the pig and her knife.

The Clear Creek episode led some people to suspect that the entire Wild Girl story was a hoax. The *Lake Charles Echo* claimed that some Alexandria businessmen decided to cash in on the story after the first few sightings.

At the time, alligators were often used to advertise matches, patent medicines and almanacs. The newspaper speculated that the businessmen got the idea of using the Wild Girl's image for advertising and hired Goulden, who happened to be a popular Lake Charles artist, to concoct the story. While the nation's newspapers drummed up interest in the Wild Girl, Goulden was supposedly hard at work creating an illustration of her with the pig and knife to use in some unspecified advertising campaign.

The *Echo*'s theory would make sense if it weren't for the fact that respectable citizens continued to encounter the Wild Girl for at least three more years. According to an Idaho newspaper, prominent Pineville merchant J.H. Hardtner and his sixteen-year-old daughter were traveling with another couple in buggies from Fishville to Pineville in October 1890 when "they saw a white female…dressed in a faded home-spun dress, and barefooted."

The woman ran away "at a speed such as, all say, they never saw [a] human being run."

The last mention of the Wild Girl the author could find was in 1891, when a woman supposed to be her was seen in upper Franklin Parish. She was described as being very powerful, covered with hair and carrying a knife or a sword. On one occasion, she attacked a boy at Lamara, but bystanders chased her away.

Because this was the first time the Wild Girl was known to be violent, a group of armed men gave chase with dogs but could not catch her. The ultimate fate of the Wild Girl of Catahoula is not known.

24

LOUISIANA'S WILD MEN

As it turns out, the Wild Girl of Catahoula (see chapter 23) was not the only mysterious person roaming through the woods at the time.

In 1860, the Bedford, Pennsylvania *Gazette* reported that a "wild man of the woods" had been captured hiding in bushes on a plantation thirteen miles below New Orleans. The man spoke French "in a manner not at all wild" and was armed with a pistol with which "he popped at every passenger along the road. Having frightened an entire parish out of its wits, a strong force was mustered to capture him....Nobody knows him, nor will he give an account of himself."

Another so-called wild man terrorized Winn Parish at the same time that the Wild Girl of Catahoula was being spotted in nearby parishes. According to the *Richland Beacon*, a Mr. Fletcher came to Winnfield to report a wild man in the woods of Ward Two.

Fletcher claimed that Bettie McCrew and her little brother were walking on the road when they saw a nude man standing nearby. The wild man screamed when he spotted the siblings and ran into the woods. Later in the day, another man spotted him again on the same road and gave chase but lost him in the woods. Apparently, the stranger was never seen again, and the newspaper reported, "Whether the man is a lunatic, or some wild human being, no one knows."

The "Wild Man of Terrebonne" was the most famous of such people, although he might be better described as a hermit than feral. Jean Baptiste Dugas was born in 1812 and became a successful Terrebonne Parish planter

In the nineteenth century, feral humans were sometimes seen living in the Louisiana forests. *Free-Images.com.*

who reportedly went insane, supposedly because his true love left him for another man. On his wedding day, Dugas vowed he would no longer be part of this cruel world and retired to a hut he built on his land. There he remained for fifty years while administrators cared for his considerable property.

Even though he had a trunk full of clothes, Dugas simply wore a blanket and slept on a pile of moss. Initially, he lived on snakes, rats and wild hogs, but his administrators finally began bringing him food, which he shared with the insects that inhabited his hut. It was said that Dugas even fed the ants by pouring syrup in oyster shells. When the hut burned in 1890, the local men built him another.

Dugas was described as a gentle man who avoided people, although he did interact with children who sometimes visited. He was not considered dangerous unless provoked and then was best left alone, because he always kept a knife handy.

The only time Dugas was known to have left his property was to attend court in Houma after being charged with destroying the local Catholic church. Dugas had donated the property for the church but became upset when dancing was allowed at a fundraising fair. The *Houma Courier* reported that Dugas was caught red-handed trying to tear down the unfinished structure. During his trial, he claimed in defense that "the place was intended for a house of worship, and not for the purpose of amusements." The jury acquitted him.

Dugas died in 1891 at the age of seventy-nine.

The following year, a wild man wearing nothing but a hat and shoes was captured at the residence of one John Falson thirty miles northeast of Rayne. Without giving details, the *Crowley Signal* reported that he had to be lassoed to be apprehended. "He had been roaming at large for some time and created quite an excitement among the farmers in that neighborhood. It was impossible to have him identified."

One of the oddest sightings of a feral human occurred in 1892 in nearby Arkansas. A North Carolina newspaper reported that a Benton man saw a "strange-looking animal" running with three wolves. Curious, he followed them and was shocked to see a teenage boy running on all fours with the pack. When the wolves stopped, he would stand up to look around but then drop back to the ground to run. The witness claimed the naked boy "was able to get over the ground as rapidly as the wolves" and showed no sign of human intelligence.

The man recalled that wolves had carried off a baby about fifteen years earlier and speculated that they had raised him as part of the pack.

25

THE FIRST MOUND BUILDERS

In 2014, Louisiana received some long-overdue recognition when the United Nations Educational, Scientific and Cultural Organization (UNESCO) recognized the Poverty Point State Historic Site near Epps as a World Heritage Site. This action placed Poverty Point in the same cultural classification as the Great Wall of China.

The Poverty Point people flourished for a thousand years between 1700 and 700 BC and occupied much of the lower Mississippi Valley. The large earthen complex near Epps seems to have been the most important site of this mysterious culture.

Poverty Point contains six huge earthen ridges that were built in a semicircle next to Bayou Macon, possibly to serve as platforms for houses. Numerous mounds are also scattered around the site, the most famous being the seventy-foot-tall "Bird Mound." It is the nation's second-largest Indian mound and is so named because early archaeologists thought it was built in the shape of a flying bird.

Most archaeologists believe that Poverty Point was the heart of a complex trading system. Hundreds of thousands of artifacts have been found there, and many were made from exotic minerals such as copper, steatite, hematite, soapstone, novaculite (Arkansas stone) and red jasper. Some of these minerals came from as far away as Wisconsin.

The Poverty Point people were the first Louisiana Indians to wear large amounts of beads, ear ornaments, necklaces and other jewelry. Clay pipes indicate that they smoked, and small owl pendants carved from jasper provide a glimpse into possible religious beliefs.

Baking, rather than charbroiling, seemed to be the preferred method of cooking for the Poverty Point people. Small cooking balls formed from clay were heated and placed in fire pits, and food was placed on top to cook. Ingeniously, the Indians were able to regulate the temperature of the "ovens" by using different shaped balls. These so-called Poverty Point Objects, or PPOs, are the most common artifact found in Poverty Point sites.

After flourishing for more than one thousand years, the Poverty Point culture suddenly disappeared, but no hard evidence has ever been discovered to explain why.

For many years, archaeologists believed that the Poverty Point Indians were America's first mound builders. Now they know otherwise.

Prior to Poverty Point, Native Americans referred to as the Archaic Indians occupied Louisiana. These early inhabitants were extended families of hunter-gatherers who wandered over the landscape hunting, fishing and gathering nuts and berries. Most appear not to have stayed in one place for more than a few months at a time, so archaeologists never really considered them to have been mound builders.

Thus, archaeologists were shocked in the 1990s when University of Louisiana at Monroe archaeologist Joe Saunders and his assistant Recca Jones studied several mounds in Northeast Louisiana and recovered radiocarbon dates to about 3000 BC. Since this would make the mounds much older than

An artist's depiction of the Watson Brake mounds. *Louisiana Division of Archaeology*.

any others ever found, the professional community believed a mistake had been made in the testing and viewed the results with suspicion.

Then Saunders and Jones examined the Watson Brake mound complex on the west side of the Ouachita River approximately twenty miles south of West Monroe. There they found eleven mounds that were constructed in a circular pattern, each mound connected by a low, man-made earthen ridge. Saunders and Jones carefully retrieved organic material taken from the mounds that dated to 3500 BC.

This time, there was no doubting the evidence. The Watson Brake mounds are nearly two thousand years older than Poverty Point and are the oldest known Indian mounds in the United States and the oldest known human construction in the entire Western Hemisphere. Watson Brake, in fact, is older than the Egyptian pyramids and England's Stonehenge.

When its discovery proved beyond a doubt that Louisiana's Archaic Indians were the first mound builders, archaeologists began looking for other ancient mounds. Two have been found on the campus of Louisiana State University, and others have been found in Louisiana and other states.

It is not known why the Indians built the Watson Brake mounds. The immediate area does not flood, and there is no evidence of it being a fortified place for protection. It does not even appear that the Indians lived there, although a possible occupation site for the builders was found some distance away from the mounds.

Why would Louisiana's prehistoric Indians along the Ouachita River be the first in the Americas to undertake mound building? That question may never be answered.

26

SEA SERPENTS IN THE GULF?

Summer is upon us, and families are heading to the Gulf Coast to fish and swim. Enjoy the water, but watch out for riptides, jellyfish and—sea serpents? That's right! If newspapers are to be believed, there are some strange creatures swimming around out there.

An early sea serpent sighting occurred during the Civil War when Union forces occupied Ship Island, Mississippi. Major H.P. Ritzius was part of the garrison and recalled how eight "monster fish" swam into the harbor during the summer of 1864.

Ritzius and a few other men gave chase in a boat and managed to put eight harpoons into one of the creatures, but it dragged the boat ten miles out to sea before dying. A revenue cutter happened to be passing by at the time and towed the prize back to the wharf.

The "fish" measured eighteen feet long, fifteen feet wide and six feet in diameter and weighed 1,800 pounds. Its mouth had no teeth but was four feet across and three feet deep. Ritzius reported that the meat had the consistency of unrefined cod-liver oil and was unfit to eat.

A photograph of the animal was sent to the Smithsonian Institution, but scientists there were unable to identify it.

In 1889, the Los Angeles *Daily Herald* reported that Captain James P. Hare of the Trinity Shoal Lightship off the mouth of the Mississippi River killed another behemoth. Captain Hare called it as "hideous a creature as ever the human eye rested upon….I found it impossible to name or classify this monster."

Sightings of sea serpents have been reported throughout the Gulf of Mexico. *Free-Images.com.*

Hare and his crew armed themselves and approached the sea serpent in a small boat. The monster began thrashing wildly when Hare fired at close range and then opened its mouth, revealing large, tusk-like teeth, and charged. According to Hare, the creature "seized the side and gunwale of our boat and crushed it as easily as though it was made of glass."

Using the captain's rifle, axes, hatchets and harpoons, the crew finally killed the leviathan, and Hare cut off the head and took it back to the ship.

Hare described the serpent as being "rusty-black on top, fading to a yellowish-white on the under part." While he was not able to judge its overall length, he claimed that at least forty to fifty feet of the animal was visible under the water. No mention was made of what happened to the severed head.

Seven years later, the *Ocala Evening Star* covered an encounter the *Crescent City* had with another Gulf monster. The boat was trolling a mullet on a shark hook off Carrabelle, Florida, when something grabbed it.

The newspaper reported, "Everybody was panic strickened as the water began to foam at the end of the troll." When the creature began stripping line, the boat gave chase for several miles before the crew was able to bring it to the surface.

After the passengers and crew shot and killed the serpent, it took a hawser and capstan to bring it aboard.

The eel-shaped animal was just over forty-two feet long and seventy-two inches in circumference. Its spoonbill-shaped head had a large, shark-like mouth, with teeth set at a forty-five-degree angle to the rear. It also had a long, forked tongue, and fins up to eight inches were on the tail.

The animal was generally brown in color but had a greenish back, which caused it to look black in the water. The underbelly was yellow. Summing up its odd appearance, the newspaper claimed, "It is a horrible slimy monster."

The creature was taken back to Carrabelle and examined by many people, but it apparently was never identified.

Perhaps the only sea serpent to be officially reported to the U.S. Navy was sighted on November 23, 1901, about 120 miles southwest of South Pass.

According to the *Washington Times*, Henry Neligan, the steamer *Irada*'s third officer, filed a report with the U.S. Navy's Hydrographic Office. He wrote, "[We] passed a large sea serpent appearing about 100 feet long. The head had a blunt square nose, and was ejecting water to the height of two or three feet from its nostrils. The animal or fish had three distinct sets of fins and a tail lying across, like a porpoise. On its back was a series of humps, like a camel. It was heading about east (true) and moving slowly." It is not known if the navy followed up on Neligan's report.

27

A SHORTAGE OF WOMEN

In Louisiana's early days, the French population was entirely male, because the colony fell under the jurisdiction of the navy department. Conditions were considered too dangerous for women and children. When Louisiana was established in 1699, the population was just eighty-two men and boys, thirteen of whom listed their occupation as buccaneer.

Most of the men were *coureurs des bois* ("runners of the woods") who engaged in the fur trade with Indians. In 1704, acting governor Sieur de Bienville became concerned that the coureurs des bois were losing their Christianity by spending so much time with the Indians and marrying Indian women. He also worried about their loyalty. If an Indian war erupted, on whose side would the coureurs des bois fight?

Bienville's solution was to bring good Christian women to Louisiana for the men to marry. Thus, in 1704, the ship *Pelican* arrived at the capital Fort St. Louis de la Mobile (in modern-day Alabama) with twenty-three women. Some were as young as fourteen, but French law allowed a girl to marry at age twelve.

The so-called Pelican Girls volunteered to come but were no doubt misled by officials, who portrayed Louisiana as a Garden of Eden filled with eligible young bachelors. What they found were half-wild coureurs des bois and crude shacks with dirt floors and deer skins stretched over the windows. Even the French marines who garrisoned the colony wore animal skins instead of uniforms.

John Law and his Company of the West took drastic steps to populate the struggling Louisiana colony. *Library of Congress.*

The Pelican Girls found husbands, but Bienville's experiment failed. The women quickly became disillusioned, because their new husbands continued to spend much of their time in the woods (often with their Indian wives) and refused to plant gardens. Food became so scarce that some girls survived by eating acorns.

To force their husbands to build better homes, the Pelican Girls launched the Petticoat Rebellion and denied their husbands "bed and board" until better homes were built. The ploy worked, but it also angered Bienville. He blamed the women for creating unnecessary problems. Bienville claimed that the young women were pampered city girls who did not want to work and asked his superiors to send only hardworking country girls in the future.

Unfortunately, the *Pelican* also brought yellow fever to Fort St. Louis, and many of the Pelican Girls died within a short time. Thus, Louisiana continued to suffer from a shortage of settlers, and John Law's Company of the West took drastic steps to populate the colony in 1717–21 after it became proprietor. In addition to sending volunteers who wanted to come to Louisiana to start a new life, Law convinced the government to deport thousands of criminals, as well.

During this four-year period, more than one half of the women who arrived in Louisiana had been convicted of prostitution and branded on the face with the fleur de lys. Five of them became the first French women to reside in Natchitoches. As it turned out, the men there did not seem to care if the women were branded, because four of them quickly married and the fifth had two proposals. Her suitors agreed to fight a duel to settle the matter, but the commandant stopped them. It is assumed that the woman was then allowed to choose the man she wanted.

The Natchitoches District, which included all of North Louisiana, continued to suffer a shortage of women for years to come. According to researcher Elizabeth Shown Mills, in 1740, approximately 50 percent of all native-born girls in the district were married before reaching age fourteen, usually to a soldier or trader in his mid-twenties. When the Louisiana Purchase was made in 1803, more than one in five people living in Northwest Louisiana were descended from female convict deportees.

Thanks to John Law's efforts, Louisiana's population soared to about eight thousand. Among the arrivals were six Ursuline nuns who landed in New Orleans in 1727. The Ursulines were dedicated to education and opened the colony's first school for girls and later operated Louisiana's first charity hospital. They also took in orphans and helped care for unmarried women. Today, the Ursulines are still active in New Orleans, and several schools can trace their origins to the nuns. Saint Mary's Catholic Church is located on the site of the original Ursuline convent.

In 1728, another ship arrived in New Orleans with eighty-eight eligible young women. Each girl's belongings were stuffed in a small chest that resembled a casket, so the girls became known as *les filles a la cassette*, or "the casket girls." The Ursuline nuns cared for and watched over the Casket Girls until they were married. Records indicate that all found husbands, even one who "looked more like a soldier on guard duty than like a young lady."

28

THE CONSTITUTION OF 1812

Today, there is more and more talk about holding a state constitutional convention to address Louisiana's recurring fiscal problems. The last time we did so was in 1973, and it was a major political event involving the election of delegates and weeks of hashing out various legal intricacies. That was not the case when our first state constitution was drawn up in 1812.

The 1810 census showed that the Territory of Orleans (Louisiana's name at the time) had about seventy-six thousand people, which was more than the sixty thousand needed for statehood. When Congress authorized officials to proceed with the statehood process, adopting a state constitution was the first order of business.

Rather than having an elaborate constitutional convention, forty-three men volunteered to write the document. About half of them were newly arrived English-speaking Anglos, and half were native French-speaking Creoles. The volunteers met in a New Orleans coffeehouse, which was little more than a tavern, and went to work.

One important order of business was to decide on a name for the new state. Although Louisiana was the traditional name and overwhelming favorite, some delegates suggested "Jefferson" to honor Thomas Jefferson for making the Louisiana Purchase. Others liked "Lafayette," because the Revolutionary War hero Marquis de Lafayette was popular among the French population.

The delegates basically copied the Kentucky Constitution and adopted ideas that reflected their upper-class values. Instead of beginning "We the

William C.C. Claiborne was elected Louisiana's first state governor after the ratification of the Constitution of 1812. *Library of Congress.*

people," for example, the preamble stated, "We the representatives of the people...." The framers believed they knew what was best for Louisiana and acted on their convictions.

In the early 1800s, wealthy, educated Americans believed that voting and holding public office should be reserved for them. Common laborers, small farmers, women and African Americans simply had no place in politics, because they were largely uneducated and most owned no land and paid no property taxes. In the framers' minds, politics should be reserved for those who made a direct contribution to society, specifically in the paying of property taxes.

The Constitution of 1812 reflected this attitude and reserved the right to vote and run for office to white men who owned land and paid property taxes. The document even stipulated how much property one had to own to qualify for certain offices. For example, to run for governor, a white man had to own property worth at least $5,000. Because of these restrictions, it is estimated that perhaps two-thirds of the people were disenfranchised.

Another example of the framers' distrust of common people is seen in how the governor was elected. The constitution stated that on Election Day the voters only narrowed the field of candidates down to two, and then the legislature would choose one of them to be governor. The voters were not to be trusted to make the final decision.

The constitution also stipulated that the governor would serve for four years and could not run for reelection, although he could run again after laying out for at least one term. During their time in office, governors were able to wield considerable political power, because the constitution allowed them to appoint all state positions that were not elected.

Finally, the constitution addressed legal matters. In criminal cases, the U.S. Constitution would be followed, as would such constitutional rights as trial by jury, right to an attorney and no double jeopardy. But in civil matters, such as marriage, divorce and inheritance, Louisiana would follow the Napoleonic Code.

Contrary to popular belief, the Napoleonic Code was not a set of laws adopted by Napoleon but rather were the French and Spanish laws in effect when the Louisiana Purchase was made. This decision made Louisiana unique, because it was the only state that followed French and Spanish laws rather than English common law. Although today most of the Napoleonic Code has disappeared from our legal system, we still see it in some matters concerning inheritance and in the principle of community property.

Once the constitution was written, an election was held. Those few men who could vote overwhelmingly ratified the document. William C.C. Claiborne came in first among the candidates in the gubernatorial election, and the legislature selected him governor. Congress then authorized Louisiana to choose a date on which to be admitted as a state. April 30, 1812, was selected, as it was the anniversary of the Louisiana Purchase. On that day, Louisiana became the eighteenth state.

29

THE SCHOOL OF HARD KNOCKS

You have to love October. The cooler weather means that another hunting season is upon us, and it's time to get back into the woods. Archery deer season begins on the first, squirrel season on the first Saturday and the primitive weapons deer season later in the month.

I have written before about what my wife, Carol, calls "Terry Moments," or those myriad mishaps I sometimes have in the outdoors. I thought I'd share some more with you this month as a warning to be careful out there.

If a Terry Moment draws blood, Carol usually becomes involved, because she's the one who has to take me to the emergency room. She got a glimpse of what was in store for her long ago when we were fiancés teaching school in DeRidder. I convinced her to go squirrel hunting with me in Whiskey Chitto bottom one warm October afternoon, and we managed to kill a big fox squirrel.

Back at my place, I was stripping off the skin with my thumb and knife blade when my thumb suddenly slipped. I knew immediately I was cut, instinctively closed my fist tightly and looked down to see blood seeping between my fingers. On a closer examination, it didn't look too bad, so we went into the kitchen expecting to just wash it off and put on a Band-Aid.

We washed and applied pressure and washed and applied pressure, but nothing worked. After thirty minutes, I finally decided this called for medical attention.

At the emergency room, I showed the cut to the doctor and asked him why it wouldn't stop bleeding. He nonchalantly explained: "Well, it's because you have a little artery right there where you sliced it. It's going to keep bleeding until we stitch it up."

I returned to school with a big bandage on my right thumb and suspect that the students at DeRidder Junior High were secretly thrilled, because I couldn't wield my paddle for a couple of weeks.

Another incident that left me bloody occurred on an early morning deer hunt. Before daylight, I followed an old logging road for nearly a mile to get to a spot where I had killed a couple of bucks before.

It was still too dark to shoot when I sat on the wet ground and leaned back against a small oak tree. I hadn't been there long when a deer snorted behind me. I looked around the tree, only to see a white tail bounding through the dark woods.

A few minutes later, I looked back again and saw another deer walking along the same trail. It was far behind my left side, but I eased up my rifle, twisted around awkwardly and saw antlers through the scope. When I pulled the trigger, the Ruger 7mm Magnum roared and jolted me to the bone.

I jumped up and ran over to where the deer was standing and found a nice five point lying motionless on the ground. It was only then that I felt something running down my nose. After wiping it off, I saw my fingers were covered in blood.

Sudden lapses of judgment can have unforeseen consequences. *Free-Images.com.*

In my awkward position, I was unable to keep a firm grip on the rifle, and its recoil drove the scope smack into my forehead. When I finally got back to the truck and looked at myself in the mirror, blood was smeared all over my face and there was a nice half-moon gash near my right eyebrow. But I got the deer, and that's what mattered.

An expensive Terry Moment occurred during one primitive weapons season when I borrowed my brother Danny's muzzle-loading rifle. It was a .50-caliber Hawken, and I was going to test various loads to see which one was most accurate. Not having a shooting bench, I decided to just rest the rifle over the cab of my truck and shoot at a target about fifty yards away.

After ramming down one hundred grains of FFg black powder and a patched round ball, I fired and walked over to the target to find I had hit it dead center. I was feeling rather smug walking back to the truck but then noticed that the windshield shimmered oddly in the sunlight.

About two steps more and it suddenly dawned on me that what initially looked like sun reflection was actually shattered glass. The muzzle blast had magically transformed some small nicks and cracks into one giant spiderweb of destruction.

I hope everyone heads to the woods in October and has a good season, but be safe.

30

THE FIRST DEER HUNTERS

S portsmen often imagine hunting deer long ago, when the land was wild and untouched by modern civilization. However, if they did have the proverbial time machine, they just might be surprised at what they'd find.

Biologists estimate that the Louisiana deer herd was between 250,000 and 400,000 animals when the French arrived in 1699. Today's herd is nearly three times larger.

In the old days, as much as two-thirds of the state was open prairie or virgin pine forests that were almost devoid of deer. Even the Mississippi and Atchafalaya floodplains had far fewer deer than today, because browse couldn't grow under the thick canopy. Acorns were plentiful in the fall and winter, but there was little for deer to eat the rest of the year.

Despite there being relatively few areas where deer thrived, Native Americans hunted them with a passion. The Choctaw even had chiefs who governed deer hunting.

Before the Europeans' arrival, Indians were almost entirely archery hunters, and the Caddo of Northwest Louisiana had some of the finest bows in America. Made from hickory or Osage orange (bois d'arc), they were sophisticated and deadly.

Bowstrings were constructed from twisted deerskin, fiber or bark, and arrows were made from switch cane, dogwood or hickory. Feather fletching was taken from hawks or turkey and were either glued on the shaft or tied with wet deer sinew.

Native Americans hunting deer, illustration by Theodor de Bry. *Rawpixel.com / New York Public Library.*

One ancient Caddo bow discovered in a burial site had a leather grip and recurved tips that would rival any longbow manufactured today. Such bows' pull were usually just forty to fifty pounds, but some archers could consistently hit targets up to 120 yards.

Hunting arrows were tipped with surprisingly small stone points. Only one inch or less in length, they are what many people refer to as "bird points."

Early French explorers noted how Louisiana's Indians practiced deer management by control-burning the piney woods and marsh country to open up the underbrush, kill ticks and other vermin and create browse for deer. Similar to modern hunters preparing food plots, Indians also planted the seeds of browse that deer and other wildlife preferred to eat.

Because deer were concentrated in certain places, the Indians sometimes had to hunt away from home. A "short hunt" entailed heading out a few miles to temporary camps and hunting for a few days. While women sometimes went along, they were there only to skin the animals and carry the meat back to the village.

A "long hunt" involved traveling many miles to good hunting grounds and could last for weeks. Usually only the best hunters were allowed to participate; the less-skilled either stayed home or tagged along to do the grunt work of skinning and butchering.

Modern hunters would recognize many of the Indians' tactics. They hid in trees and camouflaged themselves with leafy branches and eased into known bedding areas hours before daylight to bushwhack the deer in the morning.

Indians also knew the usefulness of deer decoys and often caped out the carcass, stretched it on a cane hoop and cured it with smoke. They then either wore the decoy or carried it in one hand and used mimicking motions and calls to draw their quarry near. Some hunters were so adept at deer mimicry that other Indians would stalk them.

Like modern-day hunters, Indians even used cover scents such as the smoke of a red oak fire. Forest fires were common, and the hunters knew that the natural smell of smoke would not alarm their prey.

Sometimes, standers were placed at strategic escape points on the prairies and marshes, and the grass was set on fire to push the deer toward them. Drives were also made through known bedding thickets to run deer to standers.

For the Natchez, deer hunting was sometimes a communal effort. The French claimed that the Indians would find a deer and then surround it with as many as one hundred men, who chased the deer from side to side until it finally fell from exhaustion and was killed. This deer chase was said to have been as much for entertainment as a way to gather food.

The Attakapas Indians, who inhabited the prairies and marsh country of Southwest Louisiana, reportedly used relays to run deer to exhaustion.

As long as Indians hunted Louisiana's deer with bows and arrows, the deer herd remained stable. Unfortunately, the arrival of the French introduced more hunters, armed with deadly flintlock muskets. As a result, the deer herd began to plummet.

31

DECIMATION AND RESTORATION

A lthough small by today's standards, Louisiana's deer herd remained stable for thousands of years. However, when the French arrived in 1699, hunting deer for their hides quickly became big business, and the herd suffered.

At Natchitoches, professional hunters brought in more than twenty thousand deer hides every few months, and a 1788 Spanish report revealed that hunters collected two thousand deer hides on the Ouachita River alone.

The French used a .62-caliber (20-gauge) smoothbore flintlock *fusil de chasse* ("hunting gun"). It was fifty-nine inches long with a barrel-length walnut or maple stock and weighed less than seven pounds. The musket lacked a rear sight and had only a blade front sight, but an average hunter, using about sixty grains of black powder, could easily hit a deer's vitals at twenty-five yards.

Colonial deer hunters took a heavy toll on the herd, but deer numbers did not drop dramatically until thousands of Americans moved into Louisiana during the nineteenth century. Plantation agriculture and countless homesteads destroyed deer habitat, and the use of dogs to hunt deer year-round took a heavy toll.

Rapid technological developments such as rifled muskets, double-barrel shotguns, percussion caps and centerfire cartridges also made hunters much more successful.

Even with the improved weapons, however, some hunters continued to rely on ancient methods. In 1886, an Iowa newspaper reported that an anonymous Winn Parish man could actually detect deer by smell.

It is said that, on a calm day, or when the wind is blowing toward him, he can smell a deer thirty to sixty yards. He is a popular hunting companion with the neighbors who know of his power. While riding or walking through the woods he will stop, throw his head very much as a dog does when he strikes a scent, and in this way he rarely fails to locate the deer if it is within gunshot distance of him.

Nonstop hunting by people trying to put meat on the table and market hunters supplying restaurants with venison and leather clothiers with hides began pushing the herd to the brink of extinction. So many deer were killed in the nineteenth century that their hides sold for as little as one dollar each.

In 1910, Florida's *San Mateo Item* reported that hide hunters were slaughtering the deer along Cocodrie Bayou in Concordia Parish. The paper claimed that Cocodrie swamp was "the greatest natural deer park in the world," but an estimated five hundred deer had already been killed that season.

Hide hunters, who paid just one dollar for a commercial license, were depleting the herd the locals depended on for food. "The people of Concordia Parish are naturally outraged," the paper reported. "If such destruction is continued it can mean only the extermination of deer along Cocodrie Bayou and if such slaughter takes place in one swamp…it may take place in a dozen others."

Biologists estimate that Louisiana's deer population dropped from several hundred thousand in 1700 to an estimated seventy thousand animals by the early 1900s. In some areas, deer disappeared completely.

The Shively family prepares for a Bienville Parish deer hunt, 1894. *Etta Gwynne Shively Smith.*

Fortunately, things began to change. A movement known as progressivism swept the nation and pressured the government to correct such chronic abuses as pollution, corruption and child labor.

In 1900, Iowa representative John F. Lacey extended the progressive agenda to wildlife when he introduced the Lacey Act. The first federal law to protect wildlife, the Lacey Act helped curb the market hunters' activities by prohibiting the interstate transportation of venison and other wild game.

Louisiana climbed on the progressive bandwagon in 1912 when it created the Conservation Commission and gave it the authority to regulate all activities regarding the state's wildlife. In setting Louisiana's deer season that year, the commission outlawed the killing of does for the first time, required bucks to have antlers at least three inches long in order to be harvested and limited hunters to five bucks per season. The selling of venison was also prohibited (another first), but, surprisingly, spotlighting remained legal.

Unsurprisingly, politics eventually came into play when locals began complaining about state authorities controlling hunting seasons in their parish. As a result, officials set the 1946–47 season to run no more than forty-five days between November 1 and January 10, but it allowed each parish police jury to decide which forty-five days hunting would be allowed. This became the norm, and police juries continued to control hunting seasons for years to come.

By the late 1940s, most of the deer were concentrated in sixteen parishes, but even there the herd density was just one per seventy-four acres. There were so few deer, in fact, that only 15 percent of the state was open for hunting in the 1948–49 season, and less than one thousand deer were harvested.

To improve the situation, the legislature agreed to fund a program to restock deer in depopulated areas. For the first round of stocking, conservation agents acquired two hundred deer, with half of them coming from the Texas Aransas National Wildlife Refuge and half from private preserves near Minden and Hammond. Encouraged by the results, biologists took additional deer from Marsh Island, Chicot State Park and even Wisconsin.

The stocking program lasted from 1949 to 1969, with 3,378 deer being released in nine regions. The deer population exploded as a result, and hunting improved. While fewer than 1,000 deer were harvested in the 1948–49 season, 16,500 were taken in 1960–61.

Among the stocked herd were 363 Wisconsin deer. In the 1960s, hunters (including the author) encountered large, pale-looking deer that were generally dubbed "blue deer." They were believed to be the Wisconsin deer or their offspring, but biologists disagreed and pointed out that the deer trapped in Louisiana were, on average, larger than the ones acquired from Wisconsin.

Today, there is probably no genetic trace of the Wisconsin deer left in Louisiana's herd. Mississippi biologists, who used 353 Wisconsin deer and 2,491 native deer in their restocking program, have found no genetic evidence of the former surviving today. Louisiana imported a similar number of Wisconsin deer, but their DNA was diluted by 3,025 native deer.

By the late 1960s, the deer herd had recovered enough to allow hunting in nearly all of the state, but the season was considerably shorter than today. Gun season usually opened in early November, closed for a week or so and reopened for another few weeks in December.

Our current three-month gun season is a testament to just how successful the deer stocking program was.

32

IS BIGFOOT IN LOUISIANA?

Bigfoot, aka Sasquatch, is not confined to the Pacific Northwest. He has been reported on every continent except Antarctica, and some believe he is right here in Louisiana.

Let me start out by saying that I do not believe Bigfoot exists in North America, but I'm open to the possibility that there may be unknown hominids in the vast expanses of Asia. What I find fascinating is the Bigfoot phenomenon itself. What exactly are all of these people seeing out there in the woods?

The creature is said to have a humanoid face, stands between six and eight feet tall, is covered in dark or reddish hair and smells to high heaven.

Bigfoot tracks usually have five toes, but researchers claim that in Northwest Louisiana and East Texas they often have three toes, with one bulbous big toe and two smaller ones.

Bigfoot likes to arrange sticks in strange patterns, twist and break large limbs and saplings and knock down small trees to mark a trail or stake out territory. Knocking on trees with a stick is also common and may be a way of signaling one another.

One researcher told me that Bigfoot can make sounds ranging from soft whistles and peacock-like cries to terrifying screams and roars. According to him, my family heard a Bigfoot back in the mid-1960s when we lived in the piney woods of northern Winn Parish, not far from Dugdemona River.

During the wee hours of one bright moonlit morning, I was awakened by a cacophony of sounds. Our dogs were barking frantically, and the cows

Many people are convinced that Bigfoot roams the Louisiana woods. *Free-Images.com.*

and dogs on my uncle's place next door were also agitated. Something was making its way in the dark down Highway 505 in front of our house.

It made a noise like I had never heard before or since. Starting out in a low moan, it rose to a high pitch, like a woman screeching, and then fell back to a low moan.

The next morning, I was reluctant to say anything, thinking maybe I had been dreaming. But I soon discovered that the entire family had heard it.

A month later, on another moonlit night, we heard it again, but this time we were watching television. We chalked it up to a cougar, which were sometimes reported in the area, and have jokingly referred to it ever since as the "Dugdemona Wild Woman."

When I related that story to a Bigfoot researcher, he asked, "Did it sound sort of like the old World War I air raid sirens?"

"Yeah," I said, "a siren is exactly how I remember it."

"Definitely," he replied, "definitely, that was a Bigfoot."

The Louisiana Bigfoot has even made it on to television, with at least two programs focusing on sightings at Cotton Island in northern Rapides Parish and near Goldonna in Natchitoches Parish. I hunt around Goldonna, so I'll have to be extra careful there from now on.

In 2001, the Alexandria *Daily Town Talk* covered a Bigfoot sighting in Central Louisiana after Earl Whitstine claimed to have seen one while cruising timber for a logging company. "It was hairy and looked like a human in a way," he said. "I hollered at him, and he took off running. It happened so quick, I didn't have time to be scared."

Two days later, Carl Dubois was with Whitstine on the same tract of timber when they saw the creature again. "When we saw it, Earl hollered at it, and it ran off toward [the bayou]," Dubois said. "I wouldn't have believed it."

One thing I have noticed in reading about Bigfoot is that a lot of the reports describe only unusual noises, smells, eyes shining in the dark or an eerie feeling of being watched.

Are people really encountering an unknown creature, or are they simply experiencing something out of the ordinary and mistaking it for Bigfoot? If someone unexpectedly runs into a bear or a hog in the woods where they've never seen one before, might their mind play tricks on them? Feral hogs, for example, have a distinct musty smell, and that would be an unusual assault on the senses to anyone who had never smelled one before.

And where is the hard evidence? With thousands of trail cameras in the woods these days, surely someone should have snapped a clear photo of Bigfoot if he really is creeping around. As one wildlife official told me, "The two things they should be recording are Bigfoot and black panthers, but we have yet to see a photograph of either."

THE GULF COAST BIGFOOT Research Organization (GCBRO) is the main Bigfoot research group in the South. Readers can go to its website at http://gcbro.com and read about Louisiana sightings or report a sighting.

33

BIGFOOT

THE HISTORICAL RECORD

I have previously written about Bigfoot sightings, and I admitted to being a nonbeliever. However, I find it fascinating that sightings of giant, hairy, bipedal animals predate the modern era.

Over 170 years ago, the Arkansas Wild Man terrified residents of that state. The first published report in 1846 claimed that a footprint was discovered in eastern Arkansas that measured twenty-two inches.

In 1851, the Vermont *Watchman and State Journal* reported that two men were hunting in Greene County, Arkansas, when they saw something "bearing the unmistakable likeness of humanity" chasing a herd of cattle. "He was of gigantic stature, the body being covered with hair, and the head with long locks that fairly enveloped his neck and shoulders."

The creature stopped and stared at them for a few moments and then ran into a patch of woods "with great speed, leaping from twelve to fourteen feet at a time." The newspaper went on to explain that sightings of the Wild Man had been reported in St. Francis, Greene and Poinsett Counties since 1834.

Many local residents believed the Wild Man was a human survivor of the great 1811–12 New Madrid Earthquake who had turned feral while living in the woods. Two prominent Memphis men organized a search party to try to capture him, but nothing else is known of their attempt.

According to the Ashland, Ohio *Union*, the elusive creature was spotted again near the Sunflower Prairie during the winter of 1856, and some men gave chase with hunting dogs. The Wild Man tried to flee across the frozen Brant Lake, but the ice was too thin, and he retreated back to the bank. The first man who arrived reported seeing "an athletic man about six feet four inches high, covered with hair of a brownish cast."

Although within easy range, the hunter decided to capture the Wild Man rather than shoot him. It was a bad idea. According to the newspaper, "The wild man…bounded upon him, dragged him from the saddle and tore him in a dreadful manner, gouging one of his eyes, and biting a large piece out of his shoulder. He then threw the saddle and bridle from the horse and mounted. He set off for the mountains at full speed, guiding the horse with a piece of sapling."

Twelve years later, a "Mississippi Wild Man" was encountered in southwestern Mississippi. According to the Ebensburg, Pennsylvania *Cambria Freeman*, a similar creature had been seen near Vicksburg the year before.

In the former incident, some hunters were following a pack of dogs hot on the trail of an unknown animal when they discovered a footprint in the mud. It "appeared similar to the track of a human foot, and they observed also that the toes of one foot turned backward."

When the dogs finally bayed their prey, the men "beheld a frightful looking creature, of about the average height of man, but of far greater muscular development, standing menacingly in front of the dogs. It had long hair flowing from its head, reaching to it [*sic*] knees; its entire body, also, seemed to be covered with hair of two to three inches in length, which was of a dark brown color. From its upper jaw projected two very large tusks, several inches long."

The Wild Man ran toward the Mississippi River when the men advanced, but the dogs once again bayed him at the river bank. When the dogs attacked, "it reached forward and grabbed one of them…pressed it against its tusks, pierced it through and killed it instantly." The hunters fired several shots, and the creature jumped into the river and remained submerged for several minutes.

Suddenly, it surfaced, "uttering shrieks which almost petrified the pursuers with terror. No similar sound had ever come to the ears of the men, who were all familiar with the howl of the wolf, the whine of the panther and the hoarse bellowing of the alligator. After sinking and rising several times, it swam to the Louisiana shore and disappeared."

Sometime later, other Wild Men were reported near Vicksburg and Meadeville.

What is interesting about the Mississippi Wild Man is that people believed it to be an unknown creature, not a feral human, and did not ridicule the witnesses. The newspaper even suggested that the area around Meadeville was suitable for such animals. "Throughout Franklin county there are retreats especially adapted to the accommodation of wild beasts, [such] as the high barren hills, ravines, and the dense vine-matted swamp of the Homochitto river."

34

ANTOINE DE LA MOTHE, SIEUR DE CADILLAC

The first automobile rolled out of the Cadillac Automobile Factory in April 1903. A two-seat, single-cylinder contraption, it was powered by a thunderous ten-horsepower engine.

Cadillac is the second-oldest automobile brand name in America (Buick is the oldest), and it comes from Antoine de la Mothe, Sieur de Cadillac (1658–1730), the French official who founded what became the city of Detroit, Michigan.

But Cadillac has another place in history. From 1713 to 1717, he served as Louisiana's governor.

The son of a minor French judge, Cadillac settled in Canada and married the niece of a Canadian privateer. An ambitious and rather unscrupulous young man, he realized that only members of nobility amounted to anything in colonial Canada. Thus, Cadillac brazenly created a title for himself and signed his marriage certificate "Antoine de la Mothe, Sieur de Cadillac."

Apparently, no one looked into the fraudulent claim, and Cadillac's fortunes began to rise. He acquired land in what is now Acadia National Park in Maine, and Cadillac Mountain on Desert Island still bears his name. An appointment to the French marines and as commandant of Michilimackinac in modern-day Michigan followed.

It was while serving in the latter position that Cadillac convinced Minister of Marine Comte de Pontchartrain to allow him to establish the outpost that would become Detroit. Accusations of misconduct and incompetence soon

General Motors' Cadillac automobile is named for a former Louisiana governor. *Free-Images.com.*

swirled around him, however, and Pontchartrain launched an investigation that concluded that Cadillac was, indeed, a scoundrel.

Instead of arresting Cadillac, Pontchartrain appointed him governor of the struggling Louisiana colony. Why he promoted a known incompetent to such a position is not known, but it may be that Pontchartrain preferred that to admitting he had been duped by such a fraud. Whatever the reason, Cadillac arrived at his new post in 1713 with his wife and two daughters.

Cadillac had been told that Louisiana was a prosperous colony, but his first stop at Dauphin Island shocked him. After fourteen years of settlement, the island boasted just one shriveled garden with a scattering of fruit trees and vineyards with rotten grapes. "This is the terrestrial paradise?" he asked.

Things spiraled downward from there. Haughty, pompous, untrustworthy and corrupt, Cadillac became the object of scorn when he settled in at the capital of Fort St. Louis de la Mobile (in modern-day Alabama). Fort St. Louis flooded regularly, and its inhabitants lived in small shacks with dirt floors and deerskin windows. Nonetheless, the tall, thin-legged governor insisted on wearing the large curly wigs and fancy clothes that were popular in France.

Cadillac clashed with the economic official known as the commissary and former governor Jean Baptiste Lemoyne, Sieur de Bienville, who now commanded the marines. Both men despised Cadillac, the former because of the governor's corruption and the latter because Cadillac had replaced him as governor. Bienville also claimed that Cadillac unsuccessfully pressured him to marry one of his daughters to form a political alliance between the LeMoyne and Cadillac families.

No one seemed to care for the new governor. The settlers disliked his haughty manners and the fact that he ordered the men to stop wearing swords (a symbol of rank) and closed the taverns in an attempt to rein in the excessive drinking. The Indians also became angry after Cadillac refused to smoke the traditional calumet, or peace pipe, with them.

Cadillac, in turn, had nothing but disdain for his subjects. He claimed that the settlers were lazy, violent and immoral drunkards and once wrote, "If I send away all the loose females, there will be no women left." Louisiana, Cadillac declared, was "not worth a straw."

Although Cadillac was an unpopular governor, he achieved a great deal during his short stay in Louisiana. He established settlements at Natchitoches and Natchez, increased the population and improved the colony's governing system by adopting the "Customs of Paris" as the legal code and establishing the Superior Council. The latter was an administrative body of about a dozen members that passed laws and held court.

Despite his achievements, Cadillac's unpopularity led to Bienville replacing him as governor in 1716. Cadillac's time in Louisiana is largely forgotten, but his name lives on in General Motors' most luxurious automobile.

35

THE TEXAS CONNECTION

Texas, the former republic and the second-largest state, is home to millions of proud citizens. But how many of them have ever thanked Louisiana for hosting its capital for forty-three years and inspiring its famous Lone Star Flag?

In the early eighteenth century, the boundary between Spanish Texas and French Louisiana was ill-defined. When the French established an outpost at Natchitoches in 1714, Spanish officials became concerned that their sometimes enemy might encroach on Texas soil.

Thus, in 1721, the Spanish army was sent across the Sabine River to turn a small church mission into a fort named the Presidio Nuestra Señora del Pilar de Los Adaes. Generally referred to as Los Adaes ("LOS uh-DICE"), it was named for the Adais Indians who lived there and was located just fifteen miles west of Natchitoches near the modern-day town of Robeline, Louisiana.

Situated at the eastern end of the El Camino Real ("the king's road"), the fort was perched atop a piney hill. It had a traditional log palisade but also included a medieval-style moat around the fort, complete with a drawbridge. Today, the Louisiana Office of State Parks owns the property and maintains it as an archaeological site.

Los Adaes became a settlement of several hundred people, and from 1729 to 1772 it served as the capital of Texas and was the home of the Texas governor. The Spaniards there and the French at nearby Natchitoches usually got along, but there were occasional frictions.

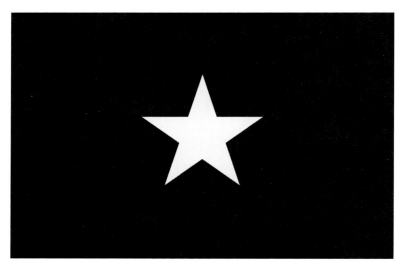

The West Florida Republic's Lone Star Flag was later incorporated into the Texas flag. *Free-Images.com.*

During one conflict, Louis Juchereau de St. Denis, the commandant of Natchitoches, raided Los Adaes. When he discovered there were only three Spanish soldiers at the fort, however, he was content to just steal their chickens and return home, ending what became known as the "Chicken War."

On another occasion, a Frenchman fell in love with the Spanish commandant's granddaughter and ran off with her to get married. The Spanish thought she was kidnapped and threatened to attack Natchitoches, but St. Denis proved that the girl had willingly eloped, and the crisis passed.

After Spain acquired Louisiana in 1763, officials realized that Los Adaes was superfluous, as there was no longer a need to guard the border, and Natchitoches had become a larger and more thriving community. Thus, the capital of Texas was moved to San Antonio in 1772, and Los Adaes was abandoned the following year.

Thirty-seven years later, in 1810, the Anglo settlers living in West Florida rebelled against their Spanish rulers. When the rebels raised a small force to capture the Spanish fort at Baton Rouge, Melissa Johnson, the wife of one of the soldiers, made a flag for them to carry. With a five-pointed white star on a blue background, it was soon dubbed the "Lone Star Flag."

The rebels captured Baton Rouge, raised their flag over the fort on September 23 and declared independence three days later. The newly formed Republic of West Florida then adopted the Lone Star Flag as its official banner.

President James Madison annexed West Florida a few weeks later and incorporated part of it into Louisiana. That area is still known as the Florida Parishes.

When Texas rose up against Mexico twenty-five years later, some of the rebels adopted their own versions of the Lone Star Flag. One that was used in the first battles was identical to the West Florida flag except it had the word "Independence" emblazoned across the bottom. Other Lone Star Flags showed up later when Louisiana volunteers began to arrive.

Various Lone Star Flags of different designs continued to be used during Texas's revolutionary period, including its first official flag. It was a copy of the West Florida banner except the star was yellow rather than white.

When Texas's modern-day flag was designed in 1838–39, the committee members incorporated the white star on blue background that flew over Baton Rouge, and the Texas Lone Star Flag was born.

West Florida's Lone Star Flag eventually became known as the Bonnie Blue Flag and was adopted by secessionists during the Civil War period. It was, in fact, the first flag raised over the Mississippi capitol building when that state seceded in 1861. Harry McCarthy was so moved by the scene that he penned a song titled "The Bonnie Blue Flag."

As a result, the Bonnie Blue Flag became almost as popular as the Confederate battle flag during the Civil War and is even referred to in the movie *Gone with the Wind*. When Rhett Butler holds his daughter for the first time, he names her Bonnie because "her eyes are as blue as the Bonnie Blue Flag."

36

RULES FOR THE ROAD

C arol and I love to travel, and by that I mean hopping into the truck and driving several thousand miles just to see new country. Our personal best was a twenty-one-day, 7,500-mile road trip to the Pacific Northwest, and we never spent more than one night in the same motel.

I should also mention that I do all of the driving. I truly enjoy it, and Carol certainly enjoys letting me.

Surviving such trips and still be on talking terms at the end requires a routine. Over the years, I have developed some rules that work well for us. So, here are my rules for the road.

1. Never pass up an opportunity to go to the bathroom. On just about every trip, we find ourselves stuck on the road because of wrecks or construction. Once you leave the gas station, it's a crapshoot as to when you'll be able to stop at another one. This rule becomes even more important the older you get.

2. Make a short stop every one hundred miles to stretch your legs. Sure, I can drive a lot longer than that before stopping, but why should I? The whole point of the trip is to enjoy yourself, and it's fun to stop at a funky roadside gas station/gift shop/diner/sporting-goods store and spend ten minutes looking around. Making regular, short stops will keep you alert, reduce aches and cramps and give you something to look forward to.

3. Eat a big breakfast and dinner—skip lunch. Most motels serve a free breakfast. Some are just a continental breakfast with the ubiquitous waffle maker, but many serve a full, hot meal. By eating at the motel, you

Following ten simple rules can make your driving vacation more enjoyable. *Author's collection.*

save a lot of money and avoid the midafternoon drowsiness that inevitable sets in after a big lunch. There's nothing more miserable, or dangerous, than trying to drive when all you really want to do is take a nap.

4. Eat all of your bacon. I adopted this rule when our youngest daughter, Amie, was traveling with us in Oregon and didn't want all of her bacon. Never, ever leave bacon on your plate. The chickens just donated the eggs, but the pigs made a sacrifice, and you have to respect that.

5. Get off the interstate occasionally. Turn off the GPS, get out the map and look for historical sites, museums and natural wonders on roads that go in the general direction you are traveling. One of our memorable trips was taking an impromptu detour through Idaho's Thousand Springs Valley, where beautiful waterfalls literally shoot out of the basalt cliffs. On another occasion, in Arizona, we left the interstate and drove along Route 66 and saw some old Burma Shave signs.

6. Don't let your gas tank get below half full. We once drove along a stretch of Highway 6 in Nevada where it was 175 miles between gas stations.

Luckily, I had filled the tank at our last stop. Keeping your tank topped off is a good habit to develop, especially in the West, where gas stations can be few and far between.

7. If possible, do not go back the same way you came. This is just a habit I have always had. Why go back the same way when you can go another way and see new country? On a side note, I find it interesting that General Ulysses S. Grant had this same trait.

8. Take a break from the restaurant chains and try out the small diners where all of the trucks are parked. That being said, this old rule is not foolproof. The lunch menu for one popular restaurant in Iowa offered a meat and two sides, but three of the four sides were potato dishes.

9. Unless absolutely necessary, don't be tied down by reservations. Admittedly, there have been a few nights when we had a hard time finding a room—like the time there was a motorcycle rally in Fort Smith, Arkansas, and the weekend in Minnesota when even the local folks were on the road looking at the autumn leaves. But usually it works out well and gives you the freedom to drive at your own pace without worrying about getting somewhere at a specific time. Invest a few dollars in *The Next Exit*, a book and a phone app that lists motels, restaurants and other points of interest at exits on major roads in each state.

10. When you start getting tired in the afternoon, put on Mary Chapin Carpenter's "Down at the Twist and Shout" and Crank 'er up!

37

THE MIGHTY RED

Today, the beautiful Red River is a fishing mecca and a sportsman's paradise, but until fairly recently, it was one of the nation's last untamed rivers.

For most of recorded history, the mighty Red has posed problems for Louisianians. Its geological quirks made it an oddity among Louisiana streams, and its murky water could be downright treacherous.

Fed by two branches in the Texas Panhandle, the Red River is Louisiana's second-largest stream. It flows 1,360 miles across the border of Texas and Oklahoma, through Southwest Arkansas and across North Louisiana to empty into the Atchafalaya River near Simmesport.

Reddish sediment suspended in the water gives the river its name. More than two hundred years ago, explorer C.C. Robin claimed that local inhabitants believed the muddy water had special powers, perhaps because of the rich farmland that lay along its banks. "They attribute to it the capacity for increasing fertility…and especially of increasing the frequency of the occurrences of triplets."

Early explorers such as Robin discovered that the Red River was unique in three ways. First was the water's peculiar salty taste. Around 1800, both Robin and fellow explorer James Pitot wrote that it was "brackish," and Pitot claimed one could barely drink it when the river was low.

Both men correctly identified an underground salt dome as the culprit. Far upstream on the Texas-Oklahoma border, the river flows over a salt dome and picks up just enough salt to make the water sometimes brackish.

This salt content frustrated Louisiana farmers for generations, because crops do not tolerate salt well. If farmers regularly used Red River water for irrigation, they were slowly killing their fields.

The Red River was also the only major river in Louisiana that had whitewater rapids. Over eons of time, it cut through a formation of sandstone at modern-day Alexandria and created a series of rapids that stretched for nearly a mile. When French explorers encountered the rapids, they named the area (and later parish) Rapides.

Just upstream from the rapids was the river's third unusual feature. A huge logjam called the Great River Raft clogged the Red and made boat passage impossible. Starting around Boyce, it stretched for perhaps 150 miles upstream.

Eventually, both the raft and rapids were removed, but the Red continued to taunt farmers, because they could not use its salty water for irrigation. Sportsmen also found little use for the river, because the heavy sediment made it difficult for any fish other than catfish to survive.

Businessmen were more concerned about using the river for commercial traffic. Unfortunately, despite the clearing of the raft and the cutting of a channel through the rapids, the Red remained so shallow during the summer that it was impossible for barges to go beyond Alexandria.

Red River. *Author's collection.*

By the late twentieth century, the Red was the largest undammed river in the United States. Shreveport and Bossier City sat on the bank of the second-largest river in Louisiana but were unable to tap it for commercial transportation.

To correct this, the Louisiana legislature created the Red River Waterway Commission in the mid-1960s to work with Congress to make the river navigable all the way to Shreveport. As it turned out, Louisiana at that time had some of the nation's most powerful politicians, including Senator J. Bennett Johnston.

Johnston pushed a plan to build five locks and dams on the river, and in the 1980s, he helped convince Congress to appropriate approximately $2 billion for the project. Completed in 1994, the newly dammed river was named the J. Bennett Johnston Waterway.

The locks and dams created five pools and a 9-foot-deep and 200-foot-wide channel from Shreveport–Bossier City to near the Mississippi River. The locks are 84 feet wide, 705 feet long and provide 141 feet of lift.

The dams also help control flooding and allow both the salt and sediment to settle to the river bottom by slowing the current. Water quality has greatly improved, and many fish species now thrive in the pools. Today, the Red River is one of the most popular fishing spots in the South, and many farmers are using its water for irrigation.

The federal government also enhanced Northwest Louisiana's recreational potential by creating a federal wildlife preserve along the river. In 2001, the Red River National Wildlife Refuge Act was signed to create a federal wildlife refuge containing approximately fifty thousand acres along the river between Colfax and the Arkansas state line. It culminates more than 150 years of trying to tame the mighty Red River.

38

THE FREEMAN-CUSTIS EXPEDITION

E arly Louisiana explorers, settlers and traders regularly used the Red River to move back and forth between Natchitoches and New Orleans, but it was not until the early nineteenth century that the river was seriously explored.

President Thomas Jefferson ordered the first expedition up the Red, and on April 19, 1806, Thomas Freeman and Peter Custis led twenty-two men, two flat-bottomed boats and a pirogue out of Fort Adams, Mississippi. More soldiers and guides were picked up later.

After navigating the river's treacherous mouth, the men soon noticed watermarks fourteen to twenty feet high on the trees. Freeman later witnessed the floods himself and wrote, "[F]ew men can be found hardy enough to stand the poisonous effects of Half dried mud, putrid fish & Vegetable matter—almost impregnable cane brakes, and swarms of mosketos—with which these low lands abound after the waters are withdrawn."

Portaging around the rapids at modern-day Alexandria, the expedition reached a fork in the river near modern-day Boyce where the logjam known as the Great River Raft began.

The western fork was called Cane River because of the numerous cane brakes along its banks. The eastern fork was considered to be the main Red River channel, but local inhabitants called it the Riviére de Petit Bon Dieu (River of the Little Good God). The name was said to be a reference to a priest losing his "images" there years earlier. Although the circumstances are not known, he may have lost a small statue of the baby Jesus that Catholics often possess.

President Thomas Jefferson ordered the first scientific exploration of the Red River. *Library of Congress*.

Guides informed Freeman and Custis that the Riviére de Petit Bon Dieu was too clogged with logs to pass through. As a result, they entered Cane River and headed toward Natchitoches.

Paddling up Cane River, the expedition began to encounter more and more people. Freeman wrote, "The inhabitants are a mixture of French, Spanish, Indian, and Negro blood, the latter often predominating, and live in small cottages on the banks and near the river."

After passing Natchitoches, the men reconnected with the Red River just below the high bluffs known as Grand Ecore. When they reached Campti, they began to encounter another series of logjams and had to detour into a small stream known as Bayou Datche.

Freeman claimed that Bayou Datche was an Indian term meaning a "gap eaten by a Bear in a log." Today, we know it as Bayou Dorcheat.

Paddling up Bayou Datche, the party soon entered Lake Bistineau and was awed by its splendor. Freeman reported, "[It] is beautifully variegated with handsome clumps of cypress trees thinly scattered on it….It is called by the Indians Big Broth, from the vast quantities of froth seen floating on its surface at high water."

From Lake Bistineau, the men encountered a labyrinth of sloughs, lakes and bayous they called the "Great Swamp." One of the bodies of water was known as Swan Lake and may have been located south of modern-day Bossier City. Some years later, another explorer noted that there were a large number of huge alligators in this lake that "roared like great bulls."

One of the most difficult stretches of water for the men was Red Chute Bayou in Bossier Parish. Its current was so swift that they had to tie ropes onto trees and bushes and pull the boats upstream. Increasing the danger was a large number of dead trees that came crashing down whenever a boat bumped them.

From Red Chute Bayou, the boats entered an area Custis called "Badtka," which may have been modern-day Bodcau Swamp. Freeman claimed that extreme care was taken not to run into the many dead trees that also littered that passageway. In some places, the vegetation also crowded around the boats so thick that the men could barely see beyond the boats' bows.

After much difficulty, the expedition finally made it to modern-day Swan Lake and then reentered the Red River by way of Willow Chute near Benton. While visiting the Coushatta Indians who lived in the area, Freeman wrote, "Cat Fish were taken at the camp near the village, of from 15 to 70 pounds weight."

From the Coushatta village, Freeman and Custis continued upstream into Arkansas and points west. However, they never made it to the river's headwaters, because Spanish authorities in Mexico sent soldiers to intercept them in what is now Bowie County, Texas. In August 1806, the expedition was forced to turn around and head back. Despite their failure to complete the mission, Freeman and Custis made the first scientific study of the Red River.

SEE DAN FLORES, ED. *Jefferson and Southwestern Exploration: Freeman and Custis Accounts of the Red River Expedition of 1806.* Norman: University of Oklahoma Press, 1984.

39

THE SPANISH TOUCH

Louisiana's French heritage is well known, much more so than our Spanish traditions.

While it is true that Spain ruled over Louisiana (1763–1800) for about half as long as the French did, and few Spanish people settled here during that time, the Spanish did make a significant impact on our culture.

The Spanish particularly affected western Louisiana. When the French established an outpost at Natchitoches in 1714, the Spanish retaliated a few years later with their own fort at Los Adaes in modern-day Sabine Parish. Los Adaes not only served as the capital of Spanish Texas but also influenced the entire region.

One example of this legacy is today's Choctaw-Apache Indian tribe of Ebarb. The Apaches are native to the Desert Southwest, and they frequently fought the Spanish in the eighteenth century. Many captured Apaches were sold as slaves to the Spanish at Los Adaes, who in turn often sold them to the French in Natchitoches.

Later in the eighteenth century, Choctaw Indians from Mississippi migrated to Louisiana and married the Apaches. The descendants of those unions went on to form Louisiana's Choctaw-Apache tribe.

When Los Adaes was abandoned in 1773, some of the Spanish inhabitants refused to move and scattered into the woods. Many people who live in Sabine Parish today can trace their ancestry to these early settlers.

Until recently, a unique Spanish dialect could be found in and around the town of Zwolle, home of the popular annual Tamale Festival. Because the

New Orleans' "Cities of the Dead" reflect Spanish cultural practices. *Free-Images.com.*

Spaniards who lived in the Los Adaes area were completely isolated from other Spanish settlements, the language never evolved as it did in the rest of New Spain. The Spanish dialect found around Zwolle was eighteenth-century Mexican Spanish, and it did not exist anywhere else in the world.

Unfortunately, the number of Spanish speakers in western Louisiana has dwindled in modern times. Dr. Charles Holloway, a professor of foreign languages at the University of Louisiana at Monroe, recorded and documented the dialect, but it is questionable if anyone is still fluent in it.

Interestingly, Dr. Holloway studied another unusual Spanish dialect in southeastern Louisiana. Among the Spaniards who moved to Louisiana during the late eighteenth century were several thousand Canary Islanders. Known as Isleños ("eece-LAYN-yohs"), or "islanders," they settled in modern-day St. Bernard, Ascension and Plaquemines Parishes.

Today, the Isleños still live in southeast Louisiana and carry on their traditional crafts. Some also speak a unique Spanish dialect called Brule ("BROO-lee"). Sadly, like the Spanish dialect around Zwolle, this language is slowly dying out as the older Isleños pass away. In addition, Hurricane Katrina devastated the Isleños communities and dispersed many of the people.

Spanish influence can also be seen today in New Orleans. One enduring myth about the Crescent City is that the cemeteries' above-ground vaults were used because the high water table made it impossible to bury bodies. Actually, this is only partly true.

The city used regular graves throughout the French period. While there were some problems with the high water table, that is not why the so-called Cities of the Dead exist. The use of aboveground vaults, such as can be found in St. Louis Cemetery, is simply a Spanish cultural trait that became popular with the city's residents.

Today, 90 percent of the graves in New Orleans are aboveground vaults. This is the highest percentage of any city in the world.

Tourists and residents of New Orleans' French Quarter can also thank the Spanish for the Vieux Carré's unique architecture. Two devastating fires in 1788 and 1794 burned down nearly the entire city (two hurricanes also flattened it between the fires).

Prior to 1794, the buildings of New Orleans were made mostly of wood and reflected French architecture. But when rebuilding the city after the 1794 fire, Governor Carondelet ordered brick be used for any new buildings taller than one story, because brick would withstand fire better.

The new buildings reflected Spanish tastes, so most of today's French Quarter architecture is actually Spanish or early American, not French. The only building in New Orleans that was built during the French period is the Ursuline Convent. The house known as Madame John's Legacy is a French Creole design, but it was built during Spanish rule after the 1789 fire.

SEE CHARLES E. HOLLOWAY. *Dialect Death: The Case of Brule Spanish*. Amsterdam, Netherlands: John Benjamins Publishing, 1997.

40

LOST IN PARADISE

It was one of the most unsettling moments in my fifty-plus years of hunting. In thirty minutes, I had gone from standing in a familiar place to being completely turned around.

My cousin Clay and I were crow-hunting on a wildlife management area and had set up at one of our regular spots on either side of an ATV trail. After a few minutes of fruitless calling, I headed back to the trail but decided to skirt around a briar patch. Then I hit more briars and went around them, too.

Knowing Clay was waiting, I moved quickly and kept angling back to where the trail should be. Unfortunately, it was overcast with no prevailing wind, and there were no discernible features in the woods. My internal compass failed me.

It finally hit me with a jolt that I was not going to find the trail and that I didn't know in which direction to walk. I yelled loudly but heard nothing in response. I then fired my shotgun and heard Clay respond in kind—in the opposite direction I was heading.

When we reunited, I discovered that my mishap could have been avoided if I had simply looked at a map. The reason I couldn't find the ATV trail was that I assumed it continued straight from my original position; it actually made a sharp turn away from me.

Hunting season is upon us, and while most hunters take precautions to avoid mishaps with their guns, climbing stands and boats, few ever consider that they might get lost. Yet it happens every year, even though some simple steps can reduce the possibility.

Every outdoor enthusiast should take precautions to avoid getting lost. *Author's collection.*

Most cases of lost hunters occur in the woods, but it is also easy to get turned around on the water. I use a pirogue to hunt duck and deer on Dugdemona River and Saline Bayou. The sloughs are my highways that I use to get from point A to point B, but when the entire bottom goes under water, it sometimes is difficult to tell where the channels flow. One trick I've learned to keep my bearings is to look for cypress trees, particularly a line of them, because they tend to grow along the banks of streams.

I also pay attention to the current's direction. Once when paddling down an unfamiliar slough, I suddenly noticed that I was heading upstream. The slough had made a ninety-degree turn that I didn't notice in the flooded timber, and I had continued paddling up an intersecting slough. If the current suddenly changes, you know you've made a wrong turn and need to backtrack.

Keeping your bearings in the marsh can be equally difficult, because there are few distinguishable features, and the water's current changes with the tide. To avoid getting lost, take a minute before launching and scan the horizon for visible landmarks such as telephone lines and water towers.

To avoid getting lost, follow these eight commonsense rules.

1. Have a plan. Let someone know where you are going and what time you plan to be back. Remember, if you don't tell someone, no one will know that you're missing.

2. Be specific. Don't just say you're going hunting at the deer lease. Explain where you'll park or launch your boat and what area you intend to hunt or fish.

3. Be prepared. Carry more than one tool to help find your way back to the truck. For example, take a GPS unit as well as your cellphone.

4. Charge your phone. Having a cellphone doesn't do much good if the battery dies. Make sure it is fully charged, and take an extra battery for your GPS unit.

5. Protect your gear. Make sure your electronic devices are kept in a plastic bag or other waterproof container, even if you are not in a boat. You might get caught in a heavy downpour or fall in a creek.

6. Take a compass. Every outdoorsman should learn how to use a compass and carry one, even if they have electronic gear. GPS reception can be poor in thick foliage, and many hunting and fishing spots are outside cellphone service. A compass always has reception, never runs down and rarely breaks.

7. Study a map. Get familiar with the area you plan to hunt or fish by studying a map or Google Earth. Learn the location of roads, pipelines, creeks and the direction of water flow.

8. Stay put. If all of your precautions fail and you find yourself hopelessly lost, hunker down and wait. If you continue to wander around aimlessly, searchers will have a more difficult time finding you.

Be careful out there.

41

HISTORIC HUNTERS

L ouisianians have been hunting ever since the first people wandered into this area more than ten thousand years ago. The earth was locked in the Ice Age at that time, and Sportsman's Paradise looked much different from today. Large rivers like the Mississippi and Red did not exist yet, and vast expanses of grassland covered the state. Huge megafauna such as mastodons, horses, camels, sabertooth tigers and big-horned bison roamed the land.

Louisiana's original inhabitants are known as Paleo Indians, and they hunted these strange beasts, although we know little about their hunting techniques. Most likely, they ambushed the megafauna from close range and repeatedly stuck them with spears tipped with stone points.

Clovis points are a diagnostic point for the Paleo period. These thin spear points are shaped like willow leaves and appear to have been designed for stabbing, withdrawing and stabbing again.

Evidence of these hunts are sometimes found. When construction workers uncovered a mastodon skeleton in Lafayette a number of years ago, archaeologists found two beautifully made Paleo spear points lying nearby. Farther north, an acquaintance of mine found a deeply buried Clovis point in Winn Parish lying near an Ice Age horse tooth.

When climate change ended the Ice Age approximately 6000 BC, the megafauna died out and the myriad animals we see today replaced them. Forced to change, as well, the Paleo Indians evolved into what are known as the Archaic Indians. A hunter-gathering strategy worked better in the

Native American using an atlatl. *Louisiana Division of Archaeology.*

new world, and the Indians survived by hunting, fishing and gathering nuts, shellfish and berries.

The atlatl was the Archaic Indians' preferred weapon. About eighteen inches in length, it has a grip on one end and a bone or antler hook on the other. The back of a dart, which looks like an oversized arrow, is inserted into the hook, and the dart and atlatl are held together in the hunter's hand. The hunter extends his arm far behind his head (like a pitcher winding up for a throw) and swings the atlatl overhead, releasing the dart. An atlatl dart travels much farther and faster than a thrown spear. (To see an atlatl in action, go to https://www.cbc.ca/news/canada/north/yukon-atlatl-ice-patches-1.4809947.)

Atlatl darts were made differently from Paleo spear points. Instead of being streamlined for stabbing, they tend to have barbs and shoulders on them. These were probably added to make the point stay in the animal and bleed them out as they ran. The vast majority of what are generically called "arrowheads" are actually atlatl points.

Around 2000 BC, Louisiana Indians entered the Neo cultural phase and slowly began developing permanent villages and agriculture. Out of this culture evolved the Caddo, Choctaw, Natchez, Chitimacha, Houma and other historic Indian tribes who largely replaced the atlatl with the bow and arrow.

While we may never know the exact hunting techniques used by the Paleo and Archaic Indians, we know a lot about the historic Indians, because French and Spanish explorers encountered them and recorded what they saw. No doubt, these Indians were using many of their ancestors' hunting tactics.

All historic Indians had great respect for nature. They believed that man was a part of the natural environment, just like the animals he hunted, and revered them for helping to sustain life. Many Indians said a prayer over their felled prey to thank it for its sacrifice and to ask for forgiveness. The Choctaw even had chiefs who governed deer hunting.

Indian tribes also revered animals for religious reasons. As a result, some avoided certain species that they considered sacred. The Houma, for example, did not eat crawfish, because it was their tribal totem, and the Koasati (Coushatta) did not eat deer or turkey.

The explorers were surprised at how Indians purposefully manipulated the environment with fire—much like today's controlled burns in the piney woods and marsh country. Annual burnings cleared the underbrush, killed ticks and other vermin and created browse for deer.

Everywhere they went, the explorers marveled at how much of Louisiana resembled an open European park.

Similar to modern hunters using food plots to supplement the animals' nutrition, Indians also planted the seeds of plants that deer and other wildlife liked to eat.

The Indians were also protective of their hunting grounds, just like today's hunting club members. At modern-day Baton Rouge, the Houma and Bayougoula erected a red pole (*baton rouge* in French) to separate their respective hunting lands. A Frenchman noted, "These two nations were so jealous of the hunting in their territories that they would shoot at any of their neighbors whom they caught hunting beyond the limits marked by the red post."

42

OLD SCHOOL HUNTING

W hen European explorers first entered Louisiana in the sixteenth century, they encountered many different Indian tribes who lived off the land's great bounty. Farming supplied the bulk of the Indians' diet, but they continued to hunt for both food and recreation (see "The First Deer Hunters," chapter 30).

The French left many accounts of the Indians' hunting techniques. Bears, for example, were often targeted while the females were denned up in hollow trees. One Frenchman who witnessed a hunt claimed the Indians first cut a tree against the den so a man could shinny up and toss a lighted torch into the hollow. When the groggy bear backed out of its hole, the Indians shot it with a musket.

"This is a very dangers kind of hunting," the Frenchman wrote, "for, although wounded sometimes by three or four shots from a gun, this animal still will not fail to charge the first person he meets, and with one single blow of tooth and claw, he will tear you to pieces instantly. There are bears as big as coach horses and so strong that they can very easily break a tree as big as one's height."

Alligators were another dangerous quarry. They were killed by ramming a sharpened sapling down their open mouth into the gullet. The Indians then flipped the gator over to expose the soft underbelly and dispatched it with a spear.

Buffalo were a favorite pursuit in the many prairies that dotted Louisiana. French accounts indicate that the Indians either quietly stalked the buffalo or

Native Americans hunting alligators, illustration by Theodor de Bry. *Rawpixel.com / New York Public Library.*

used fire to drive them into ambush points. When using the latter technique, the entire tribe would surround a herd and set fire to the prairie grass, being careful to leave a few escape corridors open. The buffalo were then shot when they passed through the openings. The Frenchman claimed that the Indians killed more than sixty buffalo a day using this method.

Many different strategies were used to hunt small game and fowl. Snares snagged raccoons and rabbits, and blowguns dispatched squirrels and birds. At night, Indians gathered at known passenger pigeon roosts armed with torches and long poles. The bright lights blinded the birds, and they sat passively while the people knocked them from the branches with their poles.

An ingenious trap was used to gather quail. First, a downward-sloping runway was dug into the ground leading to a deep hole. Sticks were then placed over the entire trap, and corn was used to draw the birds down the runway into the hole.

After eating the corn, the quail would try to fly away but were trapped by the overlying sticks. They then sat passively until the Indians came back to retrieve them.

Turkeys were lured into bow range with calls made from a turkey wing bone, and magic was used in all forms of hunting. Each tribe had a shaman who knew the precise medicine, chant or prayer to ensure a good hunt.

One puzzling discovery made by archaeologists is that prehistoric Louisiana Indians apparently did not depend much on ducks or geese for food. For example, the Tchefuncte Indians, who flourished around the time of Christ, lived along streams and in other wet environments, but duck remains are hardly ever found in their sites.

When the historic Indians did go after waterfowl, they utilized a number of tactics. Bolas may have been used to tangle up rising flocks of ducks, and there is some evidence that nets were stretched across narrow sloughs where ducks were feeding. Other Indians then jumped the ducks and flushed them into the nets, where they were clubbed to death.

When hunting ducks and geese with bows and guns, decoys were made from gourds or by stuffing the skins of dead birds. Ibis (*gros bec*) were hunted by using a wounded bird as a decoy.

One traditional goose-hunting tactic came to light only in the 1960s, when an old Indian man on Catahoula Lake caught some wild geese by hand. Before daylight, he waded out in shallow water where he knew geese congregated and sat down with only his head sticking above the water.

The man told astonished wildlife officials that geese were curious creatures, and if you sat still long enough, the birds would eventually check you out. He then grabbed them by the legs under the water. The old Indian was nonchalant about it all but did admit that the wait became difficult when the water began to freeze around him.

43

DEER HUNTING EVOLUTION

One of the great success stories in Louisiana conservation is the 1949–69 deer restocking program (see chapter 31, "Decimation and Restoration"). Deer hunting, which had all but disappeared in most areas, was resurrected as a result and quickly became one of the state's most popular outdoor activities.

In the 1960s, only bucks could be harvested, and running dogs was the most common way to hunt. Hunting with dogs, in fact, was an important community social event, as men and boys spanning several generations spent the day making drives, visiting and reminiscing.

Nearly everyone used shotguns loaded with buckshot, although most hunters carried a couple of "bear balls" with them in case a long shot presented itself.

There was no hunter's orange, camouflage clothing, insulated boots, waterproof GORE-TEX jackets or ATVs. Work coveralls, leather boots pulled over several layers of socks and cotton gloves kept hunters warm, and hunting vehicles were often the family car.

As deer became more prevalent in the 1970s, one or two doe days became common in most parishes, and still hunting gained in popularity.

In my youth, still hunting meant creeping through the woods trying to spot a buck before he spotted me. Through trial and error, I learned how to recognize feeding and bedding areas, travel corridors and transition zones. Hours afield taught me patience, how to slip silently through the forest and how to pick out a deer's horizontal body amid the vertical trees.

A lack of camouflage clothing did not prevent Rodger Jones, the author's uncle, from bagging a nice buck in 1962. *Author's collection.*

Sadly, such skills are now largely lost. Today, most hunters sit in a box or climbing stand and keep one eye on their phone and the other on a food plot or corn feeder.

Technology has had a great impact on the deer-hunting tradition. By the 1970s, metal leaning stands, deer calls, cover scents and camouflage clothing became standard, and scoped rifles began to replace shotguns as the preferred weapon. Some hunters looking for a greater challenge even turned to black powder rifles and archery equipment.

This technological change has continued. Recurve bows became compounds, and compounds led to crossbows. Traditional Hawken-style black powder rifles gave way to scoped muzzleloaders with synthetic stocks, and today even some centerfire rifles have been approved for the "primitive" weapons season.

Deer hunting in Louisiana began to change fundamentally in the 1980s, when the large timber companies started leasing their property to private hunting clubs. This was a traumatic development for hunters who were used to having free access to huge tracts of timber company land.

Leasing also led to a decline in the number of hunters and the popularity of hunting with dogs. Some people who could not afford club dues simply put away their guns, and those who continued the sport discovered that many leases were simply not large enough to accommodate the running of dogs.

Harvest records indicate that the 1990s was the golden age of Louisiana deer hunting. In each of the 1997–98 and 1999–2000 seasons, approximately 180,000 hunters bagged about 270,000 deer. Those are the best years on record.

While many hunters have reported seeing fewer deer over the last decade, David Moreland believes the numbers will eventually rebound. The retired state deer program manager says: "The baby boomer generation killed a lot of deer, but many boomers have slowed down with the harvest and it seems most are interested in only shooting a good buck. So I see deer numbers increasing down the road."

Despite that optimistic opinion, there are still some threats on the horizon that could affect our sport. For example, people over sixty make up one-third of the state's deer hunters, and Moreland sees that as a potential problem. "One day we will be gone and what was important to us does not appear to be that important to the next generation. When we hang it up, the strong support for hunting will be gone."

Other potential threats are the growing number of feral hogs and diseases. Hogs compete with deer for food, and an unchecked hog population can mean trouble.

So far, diseases have not greatly affected the herd, but in 2012–13, there were 182 anecdotal or confirmed cases of epizootic hemorrhagic disease (EHDV) in Louisiana, with most reports coming from the south-central and southeastern river parishes.

Chronic wasting disease is another threat. Fortunately, no cases have been discovered in Louisiana, although it has been found in Mississippi.

For those who hunt with dogs, the future looks particularly bleak. Because of complaints about dogs running on adjoining clubs and private property, the federal government banned dog hunting on Kisatchie National Forest in 2013, and some timber companies have followed suit.

Despite these concerns, it is still a great time to be a Louisiana hunter. Deer are found all over the state, hunting licenses are reasonably priced and we have a lengthy season with liberal bag limits. One could argue that we are, in fact, enjoying the good old days.

44

THE RED RIVER RAPIDS

When the French settled Louisiana in the 1700s, rivers and bayous were their highways. Red River was one major avenue of transportation, but a stretch of whitewater rapids at modern-day Alexandria hampered travel.

When explorers Thomas Freeman and Peter Custis reached the rapids in 1805, Freeman noted that there were two separate stretches of white water where the river flowed over strata of clay. The two rapids were about three-quarters of a mile apart, with the upper one being near the modern-day U.S. Highway 167 bridge.

Freeman reported that the lower rapids were very swift and that the water dropped about ten feet over a distance of fifty yards. In his report, Custis claimed that there also was a four-foot waterfall that had to be portaged around.

The upper rapids had about the same rate of drop, but Freeman noted that the water was also quite swift for approximately 550 yards above the rapids. In later years, these rapids prevented steamboats from passing beyond Alexandria except during times of high water.

Admiral David Porter discovered this during the Civil War's 1864 Red River campaign, when a large Yankee army under General Nathaniel P. Banks and dozens of navy vessels under Porter moved up the Red River to capture Shreveport.

When the Confederates defeated Banks at the Battle of Mansfield, the Union forces retreated to Alexandria. On arrival, Porter was horrified to

Artist's depiction of Porter's fleet passing through Bailey's Dam. *Library of Congress.*

find that the river had fallen so low that he could not get his vessels over the rapids.

Porter's largest ironclads drew seven feet of water, but the river at the rapids had fallen to three and a half feet. With the Rebels closing in behind him, Porter was trapped and made plans to destroy his ships to keep them out of enemy hands.

Fortunately for the Union, Lieutenant Colonel Joseph Bailey, an engineer with logging experience, came up with a plan to dam the river and raise the water level at the rapids. Porter was not impressed with the idea. Having struggled against the river's low water for weeks, he reportedly declared, "If damning would get the fleet off, he would have been afloat long before."

Porter had few options, however, and he and Banks agreed to give Bailey a chance. Soon, thousands of Union soldiers were working furiously on the project. On the Pineville side of the river, the dam was constructed from felled trees, while on the Alexandria side, cribs filled with rock and material taken from torn-down buildings were sunk in the river.

When these two wing dams narrowed the river, barges were loaded with rocks and sunk in the remaining gap. Even stones from Pineville's Louisiana Seminary of Learning (the forerunner of LSU) were used. The plan was to break the dam when the river had been raised sufficiently and let the ships ride the rushing water over the rapids.

Bailey's Dam proved a success, and the U.S. Navy escaped. Despite his initial resistance, Porter afterward proclaimed it was "the greatest engineering feat ever performed." In recognition of his service, Bailey was awarded the Medal of Honor.

Today, remnants of Bailey's Dam are still at Alexandria. Before the J. Bennett Johnston Waterway was completed, the old dams could be seen jutting out from the bank just below the U.S. Highway 167 bridge.

After the Civil War, officials finally turned their attention to clearing a channel through both of the rapids at Alexandria. A narrow channel had previously been cut through the lower rapids in 1854. A short article in the *New York Times* on February 21 declared: "We learn that the submarine operators, Messrs. Maillefert and Raasloff, have made great progress of late in widening and deepening the channel of the Red River, through the Lower Rapids at Alexandria. They have now a channel through the whole ledge forming the lower falls, over 350 feet in length, 40 feet in width, and of an average depth of four feet."

The U.S. Army Corps of Engineers eventually took over the project, but it discovered a layer of rock underneath the clay shelf. This greatly slowed the work, and the corps did not complete the channel until 1897—fourteen years after it began.

45

THE GREAT RIVER RAFT

Louisiana's unique geography presented a challenge to early settlers, because its wet environment and thick forests hampered transportation. Rivers and bayous served as highways, but logjams frequently clogged up the vital streams.

The largest of these was the Great River Raft on Red River. No one is sure when or how the logjam was created. It may have begun around AD 1100–1200, when floods caused the banks to collapse and dumped trees into the river, which then became snagged on sandbars. Or it might have been created by a massive Mississippi River flood that caused Red River to reverse course and become blocked by debris.

Whatever its origin, the raft grew nearly a mile every spring as annual floods deposited more trees into the river.

While the Great River Raft posed immense problems for early settlers, we would not have some of our most beautiful lakes without it. Whenever the logjam backed up past the mouth of a bayou, it acted as a dam and prevented the stream from draining into the river. As a result, the bayous backed up and created lakes in low spots.

These so-called raft lakes are unique to Louisiana's Red River and include Lake Bistineau, Black Lake, Saline Lake, Iatt and Nantachie.

Early explorer Thomas Freeman described the raft around Campti in 1805. "The first raft is not more than 40 yards through. It consists of the trunks of large trees, lying in all directions, and damming up the river for its whole width, from the bottom, to about three feet higher than the surface of the water. The wood lies so compact that, that [*sic*] large bushes, weeds and

Snag boat clearing the Great River Raft after it reformed in 1873. *Library of Congress.*

grass cover the surface of the raft." In some places, the raft was so thick that the men could walk on it.

To open the Red River to commercial traffic, the War Department ordered Captain Henry Miller Shreve to begin clearing the logjams in February 1833. Shreve was the superintendent of the Army Corps of Engineers' Western Waters Department and one of America's most famous steamboat designers and pilots.

On April 1, Shreve arrived at the foot of the raft with eight steamboats and snag boats and a workforce of three hundred men. The *Heliopolis* was one boat that Shreve had designed a few years earlier. (Shreve registered twenty-two patents as a result of his work on the Great River Raft.) A steam-powered windlass on the bow was used to pluck logs from the water and then run them through a sawmill set up on the deck. A congressional report later declared, "One snag raised by the Heliopolis…contained 1,600 cubic feet of timber, and could not have weighed less than sixty tons."

After six years of work, Shreve finished the job, but the clearing of the raft had unforeseen consequences. In addition to draining the raft lakes, the project also left Natchitoches high and dry.

The town sat on a river channel known as Cane River, but the clearing of the logjam caused most of the Red to flow down the Riviére de Petit Bon Dieu, a small branch of the Red River in the St. Maurice area. Cane River virtually dried up in the summer, and Natchitoches ceased being a major river port.

One town's loss, however, was another one's fortune. After clearing the Great River Raft, Shreve and his business partners established their own port farther upstream. In 1836, that port was incorporated as Shreveport.

Frustratingly, the Great River Raft quickly re-formed unless snag boats worked constantly to keep the debris plucked out. The Civil War put a halt to these efforts, but work began anew in 1872, when dynamite was used to clear the raft all the way to Fulton, Arkansas.

The following year, a yellow fever epidemic broke out in Shreveport that killed 759 people—10 percent of the city's population. At that time, it was not understood that mosquitoes carried the deadly fever, and many people blamed the epidemic on noxious gases that were stirred up from the river's bottom during the raft-clearing work.

During the twentieth century, government officials began addressing problems created by the clearing of the Great River Raft. Because Cane River virtually dried up after the Red River began running down the Riviére de Petit Bon Dieu, two earthen dams were built across Cane River in 1915 to create today's Cane River Lake.

Steps were also taken to re-create the raft lakes that drained when the logjam was removed. In the 1920s and 1930s, dams were constructed to hold water permanently in Lake Bistineau, Black Lake, Saline Lake and others.

46

TRAILER TROUBLE

Recently, I experienced one of those moments that remind me how quickly accidents can happen. I had just left Poverty Point reservoir outside Delhi after a fruitless fishing trip when I noticed a driver behind me flashing his lights. At first, I thought he was warning oncoming motorists of a trooper, but then in my side mirror I saw a piece of rubber fly out from under my boat trailer.

I quickly pulled over and was shocked to find a completely shredded tire. The guy stopped, as well, and said, "Man, that tire just exploded and blew your trailer fender completely off." It was only then that I realized the four-foot fender was gone. I never heard or felt a thing but was grateful no one was hit by the flying chunk of metal.

It was similar to another incident that had occurred a few years earlier when I was driving down U.S. 165. I heard a clunking noise and in my rearview mirror saw something bounce off the road, forcing a car to swerve.

I stopped to inspect the truck but didn't see anything wrong until I noticed that my trailer hitch was missing. The pin had either broken or worked loose, and the hitch had fallen off.

I would like to say such incidents are rare, but the truth is that a gremlin often rides with me when I'm towing something.

My late buddy Jim Brister found this out one hot summer day when I invited him to go fishing on Dugdemona River. Jim already had his ATV loaded onto his trailer when I stopped at his house, and he told me to drive, since I knew the way.

After about forty-five minutes, I looked in the rearview mirror, and the four-wheeler appeared to be sitting at a bit of an angle on the trailer. We decided to check it out and pulled over to the shoulder of the road. When I got out, Jim was standing by his door staring at the trailer.

"Did the tire go flat?" I asked.

Astonished, Jim exclaimed, "Tire? We don't even have a wheel!"

When I walked around the trailer, it took a moment to realize what I was seeing. We had suffered a flat earlier, but I had continued driving for miles. First, the tire disintegrated, and then the wheel itself ground down to the lug nuts.

We must have looked like a rocket roaring down Highway 34 with all the sparks that had to have been flying. To this day, I can't figure out why neither of us heard nor saw anything.

One of my most shocking incidents occurred when I was driving down a rough gravel road to put my jon boat in Cocodrie Bayou near Acme. I glanced into the rearview mirror just in time to see my Mercury motor fall off the back of the boat. It looked like a cluster bomb had been dropped when the motor shattered into a jillion pieces and kicked up dust and gravel as they ricocheted down the road.

Myriad mishaps plague the author when pulling boat trailers. *Free-Images.com.*

Inspecting the transom, I found that the motor clamps were still tight on the boat. Apparently, a hairline fracture had developed right above the clamps and the motor just broke off. All I could do was pick up the pieces and drive back home.

Another boat-towing incident fortunately ended only in embarrassment. Once again, I was pulling my jon boat (with a new Mercury motor) and stopped at a Walmart for some tackle. On leaving the parking lot, I gunned the truck to beat some oncoming traffic but didn't notice the high curb along the road.

When I cut sharply to enter the road, the boat trailer jumped the curb and tipped over into the middle of the street. Rods, gas tank, tackle box, boat seats, paddle—everything went flying across four lanes of traffic.

I screeched to a halt and rushed back to check on things, more worried about the motor than anything else. The motor was fine and still firmly attached to the boat, which was still tied down to the trailer, but they were lying on their sides in the middle of the road. As people came to a stop and leaned on their horns, a Good Samaritan helped me right the trailer and collect my gear.

When fishing season comes around, remember that such accidents can happen in an instant, and be careful out there.

47

MY MOM

I miss my mom. She's been gone fifteen years, but I sometimes have the fleeting thought that I need to call her about something.

Laura Lillian Scoggin was a Mississippi girl who grew up on a Newton County farm during the Depression. My grandfather moved the family to Pascagoula during the war so he could work in the shipyard, and Mom met my father there at a dance in 1944.

Daddy was in the Coast Guard and was smitten by the pretty nineteen-year-old. They married three months later and lived happily together for fifty-nine years.

Pop became a pipeline construction engineer, and we traveled all over the country following his jobs. It was not until I became a parent myself that I fully appreciated what an extraordinary woman my mom was.

My parents, two older brothers and I lived in a small forty-six-by-eight-foot trailer with all of our worldly possessions. We constantly moved from state to state following Pop's job and never stayed in one place for long.

Every time we moved, Mom had to take her boys to the school board office to enroll us in class and get a list of textbooks that had to be purchased at the county bookstore. Sometimes, we were not in one town long enough to even get a report card. When one school employee said there was no point in enrolling us for such a short period of time, Mom bristled and said her sons would be enrolled even if it was for a couple of weeks.

Wherever we lived, Mom always took us to the library regularly to check out books and ensured that we visited as many historic sites as possible. I have

Laura Lillian Scoggin Jones.
Author's collection.

always thought that this nurturing had something to do with me becoming a history professor.

When I was about ten, my parents built a nice home in Winn Parish, and my brothers and I started attending Dodson High School full-time. Mom loved that house and worked hard to landscape the yard and keep the inside clean and tidy.

I received my last butt-whipping from her when I was sixteen for breaking the cardinal rule of never wearing your shoes on the carpet. I was about six feet tall at the time, but it didn't stop her from giving me one of those classic round and round "You gonna do that again?" spankings. To this day, I automatically take my shoes off at my door.

When school let out, Mom stuffed the car with everything we might possibly need for three months, including pots and pans, and drove up to one thousand miles to the job site. On arrival, she had to find a place to stay, get the utilities turned on and rent a television and other appliances, all while watching over three rambunctious boys. She then got up before daylight every morning to fix Pop a lunch and always had a hot supper waiting for him at the end of the day.

When we were home during the school year, Mom was able to indulge her love for the outdoors. She treasured her flowers, garden and fruit trees, and we boys were constantly digging, planting and tilling.

Fishing was one of Mom's greatest passions, and some of my fondest memories are our trips together.

She sometimes went with me to run yo-yo's on Dugdemona, even though she did not swim and had to cross several sloughs on foot logs.

Always nervous in a boat, Mom frequently asked, "How deep is it here?" I would tell her, "Well, Momma, if it's over your head it really doesn't matter."

Because of her fear of water, Mom much preferred I let her out on the bank at a submerged stump that we dubbed "Momma's White Perch Hole." She was content to sit there on a cypress root for a couple of hours with her pole and bucket of shiners, whether she caught anything or not.

Once, a violent thunderstorm popped up, and we took shelter under a big huckleberry bush as the rain poured down in sheets and lightning cracked dangerously close. We got soaking wet but laughed about it over the years.

When Pop retired, he built a nice pond that became one of Mom's favorite places. While commuting from Natchitoches to ULM, I would stop by the house at least once a week to check on them, and Mom and I would walk down to the dock in the late afternoon to feed the fish, sit and just talk. I miss that.

48

MY DAD

Pop was a pipeliner who worked all over the United States and a couple of places overseas. It defined him as a person. At first, the family traveled with him, but we didn't see Daddy much because he usually worked ten to twelve hours a day, seven days a week.

Eventually, my parents built a house so that my brothers and I could attend Dodson High School, and after that, we sometimes didn't see Pop for months at a time.

It was not until I was a teenager and started working with my father in the summers that I really got to know him.

I quickly realized that Pop was a very smart guy. With only a high school education (which was eleven grades back then), he became a pipeline bending engineer. Daddy developed an eye for topography and learned how to use trigonometry, geometry and transits to figure out how much to bend the pipe so it would fit into the ditch.

Now, I have to admit that Daddy's intelligence wasn't always apparent to me. One of my earliest memories is when my engineering father decided he could dry out our wet firecrackers by putting them on a cookie sheet in the oven. It led to the Olan Jones version of "shock and awe" when all of the firecrackers started exploding. Momma would skin us alive if we even snapped a cap gun in the trailer, but apparently it was okay for Daddy to blow up the oven with firecrackers.

Another thing I noticed about Pop was that he was not your typical pipeliner. Many of them are loud, braggadocious, barhopping, profane

Olan L. Jones.
Author's collection.

cowboy types. In fact, the pipeline's atmosphere always reminded me of an old western cattle drive. But Daddy was laid-back, humble, didn't go to bars and, most noticeably, didn't curse. In the ten summers I worked with him, I could probably count on one hand the number of times I ever heard a bad word slip out. No matter what happened, he always kept his cool and sense of humor.

One of the most important lessons I learned from Pop was to do the job right. For a teenager, this could be frustrating. Often, after working in one-hundred-degree heat for an hour or so on a difficult creek or road crossing, we'd work our way on down the line. Suddenly, Daddy would start talking to himself about the crossing. Then he'd take out his old yellow engineer's book, flip to his figures and study them. When that happened, his crew would start getting antsy, because none of us wanted to go back and reshoot a job already done.

Finally, Pop would turn to look back down the line, take off his old dirty cowboy hat and say, "You know…." We knew then that we were doomed, because he always followed that up with, "We'd better go back and redo that."

It was just his way. Daddy was not going to leave something behind until he was satisfied that it was done right.

All of these things made a big impression on me over the years. I learned that you don't have to be like everyone else to be appreciated. Daddy didn't curse or barhop or boast, but he was one of the most popular men on the job because he was witty, friendly and accommodating and did his job well.

Some things I learned were important character traits, like don't sweat the little things, keep your sense of humor, stand your ground when you know you're right and do your best in every task. Some were more practical, like how to make a complete meal out of frozen hushpuppies and milk, how to cook just about anything on the engine block of a truck and, of course, never dry out firecrackers in the oven.

I've also noticed over the years that I am taking on some of Daddy's more quirky traits. Sometimes, when I'm trying to explain something, I find my hand jerking up and down like Pop did. I also find that I cannot get my thoughts out. Daddy's mind worked faster than his mouth, and he often had a hard time expressing himself. It would come out in a jerky, halting fashion of incomplete sentences filled with "thingamajigs" and "doomafitchies."

When I start doing that, Carol will lean over and say, "Spit it out, Olan!" I used to get defensive, but I don't anymore. Of all the people I could be compared to, I can't think of anyone I'd prefer than my Daddy.

49

THE PROTESTANT INTRUSION

From the time the French established Louisiana in 1699 until the United States took control in 1803, Catholicism was the colony's official religion, and no others were allowed. To secure a land grant during the Spanish period, one even had to convert to Catholicism, although that requirement was often a mere formality.

Of all the changes that were in store for native inhabitants after the Louisiana Purchase, few were more revolutionary than having to tolerate the horde of Protestants who began flooding into the territory.

The Baptist Church was the largest of the Protestant denominations that established churches in Louisiana, and its missionaries first entered illegally during the Spanish period. An African American named Joseph Willis led the way.

Willis was born a slave to an Indian woman and a white planter in North Carolina but later acquired his freedom and fought in the Revolutionary War with Francis Marion (the inspiration for Mel Gibson's character in the movie *The Patriot*). After the war, Willis was swept up in the Baptist movement and traveled west to preach the gospel.

Usually walking barefoot, Willis arrived in Louisiana around 1800 and, four years later, delivered the first Protestant sermon west of the Mississippi River when he spoke to a group of people at Vermilionville (modern-day Lafayette). When local Catholics drove Willis out of the area, he fled to Bayou Chicot in Evangeline Parish.

Lorenzo Dow. *Library of Congress.*

LORENZO DOW.

In 1812, two Baptist churches were started in Louisiana. Half Moon Bluff Baptist Church on Bogue Chitto in Washington Parish was the first, followed by Cavalry Baptist Church, which was begun by Willis on Bayou Chicot. Cavalry is still in existence today.

The Methodists followed closely behind the Baptists, and a Methodist church was built near Fort Miro (Monroe) in 1807. Lorenzo Dow was probably the first Methodist minister to enter Louisiana.

In 1803, Dow crossed the Mississippi River at Natchez and began preaching around Vidalia. Known as "Crazy Lorenzo," he was a unique figure in Louisiana history. Born in 1777 in Connecticut, Dow became one of America's most famous ministers. He held church services in the United States, West Indies, England and Ireland.

Dow sometimes would leave his Connecticut home without warning to become an itinerant preacher. Once, he suddenly told his wife, "I shall return in a year," and walked out and remained gone for twelve months. When his wife died, Dow buried her standing up in the grave because he said it would make it easier for her to ascend to heaven.

Dow had a haggard, weather-beaten look about him and sported a six-inch red, dusty beard. Although he was known to give four-hour-long hellfire and brimstone sermons, people always gathered to hear him speak. On one occasion, Dow stopped at a remote location, jumped on a stump and announced that he would preach there at 2:00 p.m., six months from that day. Six months later, a large crowd gathered, and Dow showed up.

On another occasion, Dow suddenly slammed his Bible shut with a bang after a long sermon and, without saying another word, jumped out of a church window onto his waiting horse and rode away to his next service.

The Episcopal Church had been established in New Orleans by 1805 and grew rapidly when Leonidas Polk was appointed Louisiana's first bishop in 1841. Polk increased the number of churches from four to thirty-three and personally established St. John's in Thibodaux, Christ Church in Napoleonville, the Church of the Ascension in Donaldsonville, the Church of the Holy Communion in Plaquemine and Trinity in Natchitoches. He also helped establish the University of the South in Sewanee, Tennessee. Polk, a graduate of the U.S. Military Academy at West Point, was killed in the Civil War while serving as a Confederate general.

Early settlers in Claiborne Parish established Louisiana's first Presbyterian church around 1819. North Louisiana pioneers were pretty open-minded, however, when it came to church buildings. Large tracts of land were sparsely settled, and it was often difficult for each denomination to maintain its own church. As a result, communities frequently pooled their resources and built one community church that the different denominations took turns using.

50

THE LOUISIANA MANEUVERS

When World War II began in Europe, President Franklin D. Roosevelt realized that the Nazis posed a worldwide threat and worked to increase the size of the U.S. Army and to train more vigorously. Army chief of staff General George C. Marshall, in particular, wanted to develop ways to defeat Germany's blitzkrieg tactics. Seeking the roughest terrain possible for training, he chose the Louisiana-Texas border to be the site of large-scale military maneuvers, with Camp Beauregard in Pineville serving as the maneuver's headquarters.

In May 1940, approximately seventy thousand soldiers descended on Louisiana and divided into "Blue" and "Red" armies to wage mock battles across Rapides, Natchitoches, Sabine and Vernon Parishes. The purpose of the maneuvers was to learn how to move large military units in combat conditions and to develop ways to coordinate infantry, tanks and airplanes in battle.

Although deadly serious, the maneuvers took on a comical appearance because of a lack of equipment. The army did not have enough tanks or machine guns, so trucks were labeled "tanks" in white letters, and sticks were used as machine guns.

The 1940 maneuvers were so successful that the War Department conducted a larger operation in August with ninety thousand soldiers. The maneuvers continued even after an unexpected hurricane ripped through the state and turned the land into a quagmire. The War Department was so pleased with the lessons learned that it turned West-Central Louisiana into a permanent training ground.

A tank rolls along DeRidder's Pine Street during the Louisiana maneuvers. *McNeese State University*.

As the war in Europe worsened, the National Guard was called in to federal service, and new Louisiana maneuvers were planned to integrate the Guard units into the U.S. Army. Once again, Louisianans heard the rumble of tanks and the roar of attacking airplanes. On August 17, there was even a clash of horse-mounted cavalrymen along the Calcasieu River.

At the end of these maneuvers, the War Department announced that three new army bases would be constructed in Louisiana: Camp Livingston, near Tioga; Camp Claiborne, near Forest Hill; and Camp Polk, near Leesville. Camp Beauregard was designated the headquarters for the entire region, and Kisatchie National Forest was used as the camps' bombing and artillery range. Thousands of workers were hired to build the camps, which helped end the Depression in Louisiana.

The 1940 maneuvers were just a prelude to the largest peacetime maneuvers in American history. In the summer and fall of 1941, approximately half a million soldiers were sent to Louisiana to wage several mock campaigns. Such future World War II generals as Dwight D. Eisenhower, George S. Patton, Mark Clark, Walter Kreuger and Omar Bradley participated in the training. In ordering the maneuvers, General Marshall declared, "I want the mistakes made down in Louisiana, not over in Europe."

Life for people residing in the maneuver area was turned upside down. Patton's tanks rolled into Winnfield, the Cane River bridge in Natchitoches was bombed with sacks of flour, pontoon bridges were thrown across Red River and three hundred to four hundred military vehicles passed through Alexandria each day.

For the most part, Louisianians and soldiers got along well; however, local residents often laughed at the northern boys who had never encountered snakes, ticks or redbugs. One family was shocked to find that some of the city-raised soldiers did not even know that milk came from cows.

There are many stories told about General Patton during the Louisiana maneuvers, such as the time his troop column became stuck in a traffic jam in a small town. Famous for his temper, Patton was yelling and cursing at the men, trying to get the vehicles moving again, when a priest emerged from a nearby church where Mass was being conducted. When the priest told the general that his foul language was interrupting the church service, Patton respectively saluted him and immediately left the area. Another story claims the wealthy Patton used his own money to buy all of the gasoline from service stations south of Many so his opponent would run out of fuel.

The Louisiana Maneuvers permanently affected how the U.S. Army fights. After encountering numerous problems trying to coordinate tanks with infantry, the army decided that changes had to be made. Patton and several other generals met in the basement of an Alexandria school and drew up plans to create a new army unit organized around armored vehicles. Fort Knox, Kentucky, was made the training base for these mechanized units that are still used today.

The maneuvers also gave birth to army airborne units after small groups of paratroopers were used to support offensive operations. After the maneuvers, the Eighty-Second Airborne Division—America's first airborne division—was created at Camp Claiborne in 1942 under the command of General Omar Bradley.

ABOUT THE AUTHOR

Terry L. Jones was born in Newton, Mississippi, but grew up in Winn Parish, Louisiana, where his ancestors put down roots before the Civil War. After graduating from Dodson High School, he received a bachelor's degree in social studies education and a master's degree in American history from Louisiana Tech University. Jones then earned a PhD from Texas A&M University, where he specialized in the American Civil War.

Jones, who has more than thirty years' teaching experience, has taught in Webster and Beauregard Parishes; the Louisiana School for Math, Science, and the Arts; Northwestern State University; and the University of Louisiana at Monroe. He also worked several years with the Louisiana Office of State Parks as manager of the Fort St. Jean Baptiste State Commemorative Area.

A professor emeritus of history at the University of Louisiana at Monroe, Jones has published nine previous books: *Lee's Tigers Revisited: The Louisiana Infantry in the Army of Northern Virginia* (Louisiana State University Press, 2017); *Louisiana in the Civil War: Essays for the Civil War Sesquicentennial* (CreateSpace, 2015); *The American Civil War* (McGraw-Hill, 2009), a college-level textbook; *The Louisiana Journey* (Gibbs Smith, 2007), a middle-school textbook; *Cemetery Hill: Struggle for the High Ground, July 1–3, 1863* (Da Capo Press, 2003); *Historical*

Dictionary of the Civil War, in two volumes (Scarecrow Press, 2002); *Campbell Brown's Civil War: With Ewell and the Army of Northern Virginia* (Louisiana State University Press, 2001); *The Civil War Memoirs of Capt. William J. Seymour: Reminiscences of a Louisiana Tiger* (Louisiana State University Press, 1991), a History Book Club selection; and *Lee's Tigers: The Louisiana Infantry in the Army of Northern Virginia* (Louisiana State University Press, 1987), a History Book Club selection and recipient of the Louisiana Historical Association's annual General L. Kemper Williams Prize for the best book on Louisiana history.

In addition to his work in history, Jones is also an award-winning outdoor writer and a member of the Louisiana Outdoor Writers Association and the Southeastern Outdoor Press Association. He has been married to the former Carol June Janette for forty-three years and has two daughters, Laura and Amie.